Extremes

A. J. Dunning

Extremes

Reflections on Human Behavior

Translated from the Dutch by Johan Theron

A Helen and Kurt Wolff Book
Harcourt Brace Jovanovich, Publishers
New York   San Diego   London

The lines from "The Spur" reprinted with permission of
Macmillan Publishing Company from *The Poems of W. B. Yeats: A New Edition*,
edited by Richard J. Finneran. Copyright 1940 by Georgie Yeats,
renewed 1968 by Bertha Georgie Yeats, Michael Butler Yeats, and Anne Yeats.
The lines from "Before Day" reprinted by permission of George Sassoon.

Library of Congress Cataloging-in-Publication Data
Dunning, A. J.
[Uitersten. English]
Extremes: reflections on human behavior/A.J. Dunning;
translated from the Dutch by Johan Theron.
p.   cm.
Translation of: Uitersten.
"A Helen and Kurt Wolff book."
Includes bibliographical references.
ISBN 0-15-129476-3
1. Eccentrics and eccentricities.   2. Characters
and characteristics.   3. Human behavior.   I. Title.
CT9990.D86   1992
302'.17—dc20   92-3782

Designed by Camilla Filancia
Printed in the United States of America
First United States edition   A B C D E

FOR TRUDY

Contents

Contents

Extremes of Faith

Extremes of the Senses

Contents

Man is but a reed, the weakest in nature, but he is a thinking reed. There is no need for the whole universe to take up arms to crush him: a vapour, a drop of water is enough to kill him. But even if the universe were to crush him, man would still be nobler than his slayer, because he knows that he is dying and the advantage the universe has over him. The universe knows none of this. Thus all our dignity consists in thought.

—BLAISE PASCAL
Pensées, 1670

Extremes

Extremes: A Mirror

IN THE MORAL ORDER of things, the human being ranks somewhere between angel and animal. The Psalmist hails man as the crown of creation, close to the angel; the Calvinist ranks him closer to the animal, incapable of virtue and inclined to every evil. In their daily lives people avoid both these extremes, but sometimes the extremes become their test or destiny. The philosopher Blaise Pascal rejects the angel-beast dilemma—man as fallen god or highly developed animal—and assigns him his own measure, sees him as a rational being conscious of right and wrong but unable to find a way between the two.

In body and in function we share many basic physical attributes with the primates of the animal world, from whom we have gradually evolved and with whom we have a certain kinship. In the comprehensive classification of nature made by Linnaeus, the human being—*Homo sapiens*—was placed among the apes. Linnaeus found little physical difference between man and the orangutang, only that he was endowed with reason, a faculty, however, that had no biological significance. Human reason varied greatly, depending on country of origin, degree of education, and other factors, and on occasion it was altogether dormant. Variations in human behavior were considered a matter of culture, not of nature. Today, too, many biologists who study the social organization of human beings and animals reject the distinction between ape and human.

They believe that the evolutionary process of adaptation and selection determines human behavior, mainly through genes that ensure survival. Thus even the unselfish act of an individual offering his life can serve the continuation of the family, group, or species. We are condemned to be what we are because that is how we survive—defending our tribal territory, quick to conform, unselfish when it suits us, ready in blind faith to resort to war and destruction. The animal has shed its coat but not its wiles; the human being is a naked ape.

Jews and Christians, and those of other faiths, do not accept this programmed destiny. They believe humans have a purpose that goes beyond mere biological existence. The fragile shell of the body—the human factory, as the anatomist Vesalius describes it—is but a temporary abode for the immortal soul. To be human does not mean simply to exist in a material sense; man is more than an animal—though something less than an angel.

But discoveries made by the great explorers of the modern era called into question the old belief in the spirituality of mankind (although the first primates brought to Europe were looked at more with curiosity than any sense of kinship). Dr. Nicolaas Tulp, the subject of Rembrandt's famous *Anatomy Lesson*, was one of the first to describe these creatures. He classified them as animals, but the division between them and us became increasingly less clear. Darwin and his successors disposed of it for good, even though something was still lacking in the transition from animal to man—the missing link, eventually supplied after consideration of many candidates.

The scientific study of living matter has in only a few centuries yielded an impressive fund of knowledge. The study of the human psyche has proved more daunting.

One autumn day in 1654, Pascal had a narrow escape as

his horse-drawn carriage crossed a small bridge over the Seine in Neuilly. Two horses broke away and fell into the water, causing the carriage to teeter precariously. Pascal looked into the abyss of water below, and that image would haunt him for years. He keeps returning in his philosophy to the unfathomable abyss, the abyss both of the infinitesimal-invisible and of the infinitely colossal, the cosmos. Both would be investigated in due course—the infinitesimal by the microscope and molecular biology, the infinite by the telescope and space travel. The true abyss has turned out to be human beings.

Biology is not much help in our efforts to understand ourselves. When we came to think of the body as a factory, it was clear that it could be regulated by medical science. But there is no comparable model of human behavior, and therefore no way to regulate it other than by force or persuasion. The gap is filled by hypotheses about what drives us, ranging from those of Sigmund Freud to those of Konrad Lorenz, and offering explanations ranging from the subconscious to our genes. But the human being remains a stranger in a world he did not create. Some see him as the shadow of God; others see God as the shadow, a projection of man. In the words of Montaigne, we sleep on the soft pillow of ignorance. Indeed, human conduct is often irrational, for all its calculation aimed at physical survival. Even survival ceases to matter when a soldier, martyr, or heretic chooses to sacrifice himself for a higher goal. The drab, everyday routine of the average citizen, taxpayer-breadwinner, is adapted behavior and less instructive than a life lived to the limits. Limits that mark the zenith and nadir of what man is capable of. Extremes of conduct speak of aspirations that transcend the personal and challenge the sanity of standard human behavior.

This book is a series of tales about the extremes of human

behavior, true events in which rational, normal people have yielded to passion, to a compulsion out of all proportion to the situation. Some of the tales have been told before, are old and familiar, but with repetition certain details have been left out and others added. In the retelling, the emphasis has been on such physical aspects as illness, deprivation, and death in unusual circumstances. There is more to it than that. The world is full of peculiar people who by their peculiarity make vital contributions. Their passion springs from a heart that is not just a muscular pump but a motivating force. Indeed, in many of these tales the heart plays a prominent role—partly because of the author's profession, but partly because of that special quality Pascal ascribes to it. As he says, the heart has reasons the mind knows nothing of.

This selection of tales is not random. The burning desire to live or die for a cause, no matter how unusual or extreme, is as pertinent today as ever. Accounts of saints and lunatics, geniuses and addicts, martyrs and criminals may seem more exotic in their historic settings than they would be in the context of contemporary society, which is egalitarian, prosperous, and middle-class, but the motivations and the experiences are basically the same. In the mirror of the past we see people who look different but whom we recognize with a shock.

Extremes also serve to illustrate human imperfections, often on a scale more dreadful, more colorful, or more heroic than anything in our normal lives, and this fascinates us. In our average, comfortable circumstances, we admire extremes or are repelled by them, but in either case have difficulty finding a satisfactory explanation for them. This collection of tales is no more than a brief biomedical, descriptive catalog of a few well-known examples of passionate behavior; it is meant to instruct and to entertain, and the reader should not expect morals or explanations. Because explanation—even when it is possible to come up with one—diminishes the event, reduces it to manageable proportions, and robs it of the disturbing quality that accompanies so many extremes. There are some whose every instinct rebels against death but who accept it in the end, with the flexibility of Pascal's thinking reed.

These tales, I trust, present a series of events that belong to the past but have many an implication for our own time. Their dramatis personae are bound together by the slender thread that connects all people and all motives. Extremes meet. My tales are a historical game of musical chairs. When the music stops, somebody is left standing, and then those who sat must face the music again. The one left standing at the end is Everyman—Brother Donkey, hesitating between the bale of angelica and the bale of hay.

Extremes of the Heart

The Burning Heart

THEY BOTH STOOD CLOSE to the throne, the young man and the girl, because of the services they had rendered. They had achieved this position by risking their lives in an enterprise that only a few months before had seemed impossible. The city in which the coronation had taken place, on July 17, 1429, was not even recaptured from the enemy until the day before. Within a few years both the young man and the girl, after ecclesiastical trials, would end their lives at the stake, the one as a murderer, the other as a witch. But posthumously their paths would diverge. The girl would become a saint, and the young man would be remembered as Bluebeard.

These events happened toward the end of the Hundred Years' War, a sordid conflict, waged on French soil, in which England contested the French crown, and which left France devastated for many years. There were uncertain and dual loyalties. For almost forty years two popes reigned, and a number of pretenders asserted their right to the French throne. Famine, poverty, and pestilence were widespread; it was an apocalyptic time, a time of menace, violence, and lawlessness.

The house of Orléans and the house of Burgundy were contending for the throne of France. The Burgundians joined forces with the English invaders. Charles VII of Orléans, called the Dauphin because he had not yet been consecrated (he was the son of a demented father and a dissolute mother), had been denied his right to succeed to the throne on the ground that he was illegitimate. But he managed to make a stand south of the Loire, the irresolute and disputed commander of a motley force with uncertain loyalties. Then, in February 1429, under the escort of one of his captains, Joan of Arc, a shepherd girl from Domrémy in Lorraine, arrived at the court, which was lodged in the Loire castle of Chinon. She claimed she had heard the voices of Saint Michael the Archangel and the early Christian saints Catherine and Margaret and had come to deliver their message to the king. Somehow she convinced the king of the validity of her divine mission: he was the true heir, the besieged city of Orléans would be liberated, and the king would be crowned in Reims, as all the French monarchs before him had been.

In the ensuing months Joan, riding side by side with the commanders of the king's forces in bloody combat, achieved that divine mission. Orléans was liberated; Reims surrendered. Noblemen rode to the Abbey of Saint Rémy to fetch the ampulla of holy oil, and the king, like his predecessors, was anointed in the cathedral as the true Christian monarch.

Then the tide turned. In spite of what Joan's visions told her, an assault on Paris failed, and she was taken prisoner at Compiègne by the Burgundians, who traded her off to the archenemy, the English. Her brief triumph had lasted only a few months, and those who had been following her now left her in the lurch.

Among them was Gilles de Rais, at twenty-five the youngest military commander in the Orléans camp, and only eight years older than Joan. He came from the landed gentry of Anjou. Orphaned at an early age, he was raised by a grandfather who hoped to add to his resources by finding a wealthy wife for his grandson. The two of them behaved like robber barons, enriching themselves, leading dissolute lives, eager for any debauchery—although in no respect was this much different from the way most of their feudal counterparts lived. Gilles joined the king's army, and as a wealthy nobleman was rapidly promoted to adviser to the monarch. He was a witness to Joan of Arc's arrival at Chinon and, by the king's command, was assigned to accompany her with a military escort—a warrior assigned to take a farm girl to war. Like the other noblemen, the courtiers, and the king himself, he was undoubtedly fascinated by this simple girl, who in her determined and self-assured manner told the hesitant and uncertain king and his retinue of swashbucklers and robbers about God's plan for France and its sovereign, and who would be in the vanguard when the armed struggle resumed.

It had not been easy for them to believe her. In the male-dominated late Middle Ages, marked by violence, war, and famine, women who wished to be heard had to resort to extreme forms of behavior, such as self-punishment, starvation, making prophecies, or performing miracles. Preserving one's virginity and renouncing worldly desire were other means to this end. Surrounded by uncouth soldiers, Joan remained a chaste medium for the reception of her celestial messages. According to contemporary accounts, she was an attractive young woman, but it was said she had never menstruated. No companion in arms was physically attracted to her. Her virginity was a symbol of the intangible and the sacred, against which biology and lust were powerless. Ladies of the court examined her for proof of her virginity, and theologians examined her for the truth of her assertions. When all these parties were satisfied, she was given command of the army, under the tutelage of Gilles de Rais.

The relief of Orléans won Joan the veneration of the populace, but she had a single purpose in mind, the achievement of her political mission. This, she knew from her voices, would bring her injury and imprisonment and make her a secular martyr, of which the Church had no need. She was quite clear that this was what her voices expected of her.

Her imprisonment, which destroyed her invulnerability and deprived the campaign of its inspiration, was a triumph for the alliance of the English and the Burgundians. The king and his vassals did nothing to secure her release, and immediately after her arrest the theologians of the University of Paris put the matter into the hands of an ecclesiastical tribunal. In a world full of superstition, heresy and witchcraft were closely related, both inspirations of Satan, a very real and much-feared engineer of calamity. The writer Johan Huizinga begins his *Waning of the Middle Ages* with a description of the harshness of daily existence, of the extremes of grief and joy, disaster and good fortune. Evil and good were like black and white, and Joan of Arc's voices could as well have come from the devil as from God. The tribunal and its witnesses saw only the black. They questioned Joan's virginity and attributed diabolical motives to her, judging her a danger to God and the people, a heretical sorceress.

The demeanor of the girl as she faced her sixty-four judges and assessors was remarkable in its simplicity. Candidly she described the voices of the angels and saints and answered in detail everything she was asked. She remained true to her visions, her faith, and her conscience. (George Bernard Shaw, in his play *Saint Joan*, would portray her as the first Protestant saint, an individual conscience opposing the power of the state and the Church.) Her accusers did not believe in her voices; this kind of supernatural experience did not meet the theological standards of the day—and, besides, she had not consulted with a priest or a bishop. She had been misled by diabolical influences. The facts that she wore male attire and had borne arms for the enemy were only additional proof. She would have to burn, since she refused to retract what she said she had heard.

The punishment took place in Rouen, in the old market-place, on May 30, 1431. Joan, eighteen years old, stood atop the pyre, tied to a stake bearing a notice that enumerated the sixteen main indictments, which included falsehood and deception, heresy and apostasy, devil worship and sacrilege. On her close-cropped head was a paper cap, the mark of the heretic. The pyre was lit, but the executioner was unable to strangle her—the customary way of expediting a heretic's death—because the flames shot up too quickly. And so, as she called on Jesus, Joan was consumed by the fire. Only her heart did not burn, a chronicler tells us.

IT IS MOST UNLIKELY that Gilles de Rais, who in the meantime had become a marshal of France, was present during any part of Joan's trial or execution. The French writer Michel Tournier is among those who have suggested that the knight Gilles profoundly venerated Joan, and that when she was executed he lost the only decent impulse he had ever had. He would in due course become guilty himself of everything she had been accused of.

Gilles participated in a few more battles, but shortly after Joan's death his grandfather died, followed by his patron and nephew, the favorite of the king. Gilles retired to his estate, founded churches and decorated them to excess, and squandered a fortune on luxurious living and on festivities and games, which reduced him to bankruptcy. The king placed him under custodial care, and he had to dispose of one piece of property after another. To escape the consequences of his prodigality, he turned to alchemy, the search for a means of transmuting lead into gold. Alchemy, a blend of metallurgic science and occultism, was widely practiced during the Middle Ages. Impoverishment led people to hope for miracles; but swindling and fraud made the authorities wary of alchemists. Gilles's alchemy came to naught, and with the assistance of cronies he proceeded to evoke a magic circle of spirits and devils who supposedly would provide him with power, knowledge, and new wealth. A coterie of aristocratic friends, servants, and women from nearby was joined by itinerant alchemists and magicians. One of the latter, an intelligent young cleric from Florence named Prelate, stayed on at Gilles's castle as alchemist, exorcist, and evil genius. He saw devils, conjured them up, exorcised them, and asked them to make gold. Gilles seems to have maintained a naive faith in all these shenanigans, which became stranger and stranger as time went on.

Children began to disappear from the town, mostly boys between the ages of eight and fifteen. Disturbing rumors circulated, but not openly, because people were intimidated by the brutality of their feudal master. Gilles's debts and the number of his creditors increased, and insinuations about occult and violent proceedings within the castle walls grew steadily more vocal, causing the bishop of Nantes to institute a secret investigation. This resulted in Gilles's arrest and indictment before an ecclesiastical tribunal, the Inquisition. The incensed Gilles questioned the competence of the tribunal and railed at the judges. He refused to give an account of his actions. In view of the gravity of the charges, the tribunal promptly excommunicated him. Gilles not only had thrown away his future on earth but forfeited his chances in heaven, and that broke him. At the ensuing trial he wept, humiliated himself, and made a full public confession. In consequence, the excommunication was lifted.

The records of the ecclesiastical proceeding and of the secular trial that followed indeed revealed unprecedented horrors. In the space of eight years, Gilles de Rais had lured one hundred and fifty boys to his castle as pages, by abducting them or by bribing their families, and all were bestially murdered, by decapitation, by being bled to death, or by bludgeoning. Before, during, and after the death throes Gilles had anal intercourse with them, and he then dissected the bodies. The corpses were incinerated in fireplaces or on funeral pyres, and the remains were disposed of inside the castle walls, in the cellars, and in the moat, all with the help of attendants and friends with whom Gilles was having homosexual relations. Victims also included boys in the church choir; but Gilles did not slit their golden throats, for the sake of the music they produced. The pervading atmosphere of sorcery, sadism, and perversion suggests insanity, but the manner in which the victims were gathered and their traces hidden shows deliberate intent, a silent conspiracy among many.

The ecclesiastical trial, featuring an unrestrained confession and a repentant sinner begging for God's forgiveness of his dreadful crimes, was brief. Gilles was convicted of heresy, betrayal of the faith, exorcism, sodomy, and abuse of the prerogatives of the Church, and the sentence of excommunication was reimposed. He confessed and repented, but again the sentence was excommunication. The secular trial, with a hundred witnesses, lasted a month. He was fined a large sum and sentenced to death, as were his two manservants. Saying he hoped his fate would serve as a caution to others, Gilles asked to be buried in a convent where other noblemen had been laid to rest. In view of his high rank, the request was granted.

The execution took place October 26, 1440, a great public spectacle meant to edify and serve as an example to town and countryside. Gilles, on the gallows, again asked for forgiveness, especially from the parents of his victims; he called on the saints; he prayed. He was the first to be hanged, and after him, at his right side and his left, the manservants, whom he had instructed to show remorse, because God forgives the greatest of sinners. Then the pyres below were lit; to be hanged and burned was a double disgrace, a twofold death reserved for murderers and heretics. At the behest of a number of aristocratic ladies, Gilles's heart was retrieved from the flames, a favor granted when the sentence was passed. The manservants burned to a crisp. Their master, after a church service, was interred with due ceremony in the convent at Nantes.

Some years later, Gilles's family attempted, unsuccessfully, to have him rehabilitated. A similar effort was made on Joan of Arc's behalf when, more than twenty years after her death, her mother pleaded on her knees, in Notre Dame Cathedral in Paris, for a review of the ecclesiastical proceedings against Joan. The sentence was subsequently declared null and void, on the ground that the indictments drawn up by the English archenemy had been politically motivated. The English had by now been defeated, the contending French factions had reached a compromise, and the country's recovery required that unpleasant memories be set aside. Neither Joan's innocence nor her sanctity were at issue, and her rehabilitation was as much politically motivated as her condemnation had been. She was remembered gratefully in Orléans and in Domrémy, where the house she was born in had become a local attraction. But her cult would be slow to develop.

She was seen primarily as an amazon, a goddess of war, a paragon of inspiration to French troops going into battle; also as an unspoiled child of nature and the personification of maidenly virtue. Ultimately, as the very symbol of French patriotism. That patriotism, especially strong in bourgeois Catholic France, which abhorred socialism and atheism, was what induced the Vatican first to declare her beatified and then, in 1920, to canonize her. A young French captain, wounded three times during World War I and, like her, a native of Lorraine, chose her as his patron saint in the next world war, when France again needed someone to liberate it from foreign occupation. The legend of Joan of Arc merges with his on the Place Charles de Gaulle, the site of that national monument, the Arc de Triomphe. It is the canonization of the patriotic spirit.

For a long time Gilles de Rais and his misdeeds were passed over in silence, but he lived on in folklore, and perhaps we find him in some of the fairy tales of Charles Perrault or the brothers Grimm. One of these tales is about Bluebeard, an ugly customer with a blue-black beard who murders his wives, the last of them because of her curiosity about what happened to her predecessors. Gilles de Rais may have been the model for Bluebeard, or it may have been a figure from a much earlier ballad or saga.

In any event, both Gilles and Joan have been variously portrayed in novels, motion pictures, and musical compositions. Speculations that they were romantically involved have been advanced to explain his grotesque degeneration, or to show that both were children of their period, extreme manifestations of the violence, alchemy, prophesying, and political and religious conflict that characterized the times. What cannot be explained by their lives, which were unique, psychiatry has tried to elucidate. The one was a victim of overpowering hallucinations, voices from on high; the other, of a sadistic drive and an unbridled youth. Pathological personalities shaped by time and place, education and culture.

WHAT IS INDISPUTABLE is that Gilles and Joan are extremes. Stripped of her legend and mythology, Joan may not be understandable but she is certainly admirable. Her trial is a microcosm of her short life. It attests to the purity and steadfastness of her faith, her commitment to her task, her courage in carrying it out, her bravery in the face of condemnation and death. The voices that drove her, of such vital importance to her and to her judges as proof of either benign or evil inspiration, seem to us no more than the dictates of her conscience.

Of Gilles de Rais, we know hardly anything good. Like many of his contemporaries in similar circumstances, he was a brutal robber baron, a despiser of all humanity, a wastrel, braggart, and bully. The catalog of his misdeeds as seducer, violator, and murderer of children in a demonic household is as extraordinary as Joan's religious valor and devotion, but in the face of such overwhelming evil, all attempts at explanation fail. Both Gilles and Joan were rejected by the Church and the world, the bodies of both were burned to ashes on the pyre, and the hearts of both escaped the flames. What really drove these two people remains a mystery to us, because the records of their trials give consequences, not causes. One becomes a saint, the other Bluebeard, subjects for oratorio or opera, novel or motion picture.

On their pyres they flare up briefly in the darkness of the Middle Ages. For a moment, in the heart of Europe and at a midpoint of Western history, they symbolize Good and Evil. The maid and the monster can be said to represent the outer limits of human conduct. We need no ethical criteria to evaluate this conduct; we can simply grade it like a school report, an F for Gilles, an A for Joan.

Were an entire generation to sit and take a final exam in morality, C would be the most frequent grade, since extremes presuppose a median. If we distribute the scores on the probability curve described by the mathematical prodigy Karl Friedrich Gauss, then in a normal distribution 95 percent of the data will fall within a statistically definable sector: twice the distance of the standard deviation from the median, on either side of that median. In such a distribution, the extremes are clearly the exception. A similar mathematical prorating of good and evil shows the same distribution around a median, and the same outer limits. These extremes are out of the ordinary but they do exist, just as a winning lottery ticket exists. It is an inevitable feature of human life that extremes appear from time to time, a Joan of Arc, a Gilles de Rais.

The evil in the world tends to strike us with more force, and more often, than the good. It is not so easy to come up with the opposites of Stalin or Hitler. Evil has repute and power; good is passive, anonymous. But the question remains: Is the good and evil in people indeed distributed by chance and at random?

The French philosopher Montaigne—who in 1580 visited Joan's house—fought in the wars of religion and served as mayor of Bordeaux during the plague, but finally he retreated to his tower to write his memoirs, a contemplative autobiography. According to him, both instinct and reason impel human nature, but reason is weak. The principal human failing, Montaigne believed, is arrogance, the presumption that through the intellect the truth can be revealed. We are barely superior to the animals, who are stronger, friendlier, and often wiser. Our senses deceive us, and we would do better humbly to acknowledge and accept our limitations. Life can be lived only by following our best instincts. We gain nothing by pondering life, since the future is outside our control. We are what we are; reason can neither change nor tame us; what animates us is unknown. This view of Montaigne is diametrically opposed to the Stoic tradition, which says that by knowing ourselves we can learn self-control and live exemplary lives, like that of the patron saint of all philosophers, Socrates.

Sixty years after Montaigne, Pascal rejects both philosophies. He shares Montaigne's skepticism about human life, an existence marked by passivity, anxiety, delusions, and shares his belief that all human institutions are imperfect. But it is the intellect, which animals lack, that enables us to see our base condition, Pascal says. All human endeavor is impeded by human limitations, and our intellect cannot lead us to a better life. We must rely on divine mercy, not on ourselves. For all his pessimism about humanity and its fate, Pascal is ready to bet on faith and the search for God as a way to escape the dungeon of evil.

Montaigne saw in Gilles de Rais an illustration of base instinct deprived of all reason—a specimen of humanity he had encountered all too often in his experience of war and pestilence, a human being who was below an animal. To classicists and to Christians, Joan of Arc symbolized the ideal existence, one in which dogma and day-to-day living were in perfect harmony. Pascal saw both Gilles and Joan as sinners seeking salvation, motivated by reasons of the heart that reason knows nothing of.

A distinguished Dutch psychiatrist, on the occasion of his retirement and after long experience with the pathology of the soul, wrote that psychiatry and psychology ought to be fully aware that there is both good and evil in people, but that the professional literature rarely mentions this, because science will not moralize. It prefers to talk of genes, parents, upbringing, environment. Evil is perhaps a perversion of good, the shadow cast by the light. We do not comprehend the human being, writes H. C. Rümke, and perhaps that is for the best. A scientific explanation might turn man into a robot.

Joan and Gilles cannot be reduced to hallucinations and pederasty, labels that signify little and explain nothing. The human being, subject to deep, dark motivations, remains an enigma, unique in his or her identity, grandeur, and misery.

Heart Transplants

THE NOTION that human beings have souls seems to have existed since civilization began. The soul appears in the death customs of the Etruscans and the Egyptians, and in Greek mythology. The primitive hunter laid to rest in the caves of Lascaux was given a leg of bison to take with him to the eternal hunting grounds.

Although the soul, the essence of the human being, continues to exist after death, it needs a place to reside until then, a workplace, a home, a haven. In European tradition the heart and the soul have always been closely associated, perhaps because it is the heart that supplies the organs and tissues with blood and oxygen—with life. But the heart seems to have had symbolic significance long before we knew much about its structure and function. It was not until the sixteenth century that Vesalius and Leonardo da Vinci charted the heart, and not until the seventeenth that the Englishman William Harvey discovered the part it played in the circulation of the blood.

The heart was regarded as the core of life even in prehistoric times. In French and Spanish caves are wall paintings that date back twenty-five thousand years, a gallery depicting the hunting of bison, deer, and elephants. In Asturia, in northern Spain, near the famous Altamira caves overlooking the ocean, lies Pindel's cave, which contains countless outline drawings of primitive animals, including one of an elephant. The creature has no eyes, ears, or tusks, but at the back of its head appears an emblem in the shape of a heart—the first known depiction of the source of life. We know the details of the drawing found in this inaccessible place from the precise descriptions of Father Breuil, a preeminent authority on cave paintings. The elephant outline, drawn in red chalk, contains within it a wide stain in the spot where the heart was thought to be located. In the rough sketch he made, this red stain resembles a candy heart, the familiar symmetrical V with two semicircles at the top—a stylized figure that has become known as "Pindel's elephant heart." It is probably a pure coincidence that the stain is in the shape of a heart; more likely, this is the spot at which the hunters aimed their arrows. A well-intentioned misunderstanding, a product of Father Breuil's art. His drawings, which can be seen in the anthropological museum in Paris, were executed under difficult circumstances. Lying prostrate in close and damp caves and working by candlelight, he copied the rock paintings in pencil and later completed the copies with crayon and watercolor. His elephant's heart is an artistic conceit.

The idea of the heart as the seat of thought and feeling, or as the dwelling place of the soul, is recent; it would have to await the advent of Vesalius and Harvey. Primitive peoples, with their limited vocabularies, often do not have a word for the heart, even when they have words for the liver, the lungs, and the kidneys. Whenever the soul is localized, it is in the bones, which are left behind, outliving their owner.

The Mesopotamians believed that the soul was located in the liver, as did the early Greeks. In retribution for his theft of the divine fire, Prometheus was chained to a rock so an eagle could feed perpetually on his liver. The Greeks used one word for heart and stomach, and the ancients foretold the future by inspecting entrails and the liver. In the Old and New

Testaments the heart has a lowly status; primarily it is where evil lurks—envy, cunning, vice, and blasphemy. Of the function of the heart, buried inside the chest, practically nothing was known; anatomically, it was regarded as a vessel that could contain both good and evil. The ancients, Jews, and early Christians attached greater value to what they called the pneuma, the breath of life, as symbolizing the soul. The transitory, invisible soul rises from the earthbound body and floats freely, returning to the place above from which it came.

The heart appears again in the medieval courts, in the lyric poetry of knights and troubadours, as the symbol of love, constancy, and also courage. The symbol had no anatomical basis; it was simply a peg on which to hang lofty sentiments. The heart and bravery, *coeur* and *courage*—and if your heart was the motivator for war, love, or adultery, you could be forgiven. It would be some time before anyone attempted to come up with an image of this mysterious organ, and then the results were modest. Heart-shaped watermarks were used in the production of medieval paper, and in the tapestries that adorned the houses of wealthy citizens young men were depicted on their knees proffering their hearts to the ladies of their choice. The heart also began to be used on playing cards, in the form of the king and queen of hearts, giving a symbolic overlay to the activity of gambling.

The heart had limited significance in medieval religion. The mystic meditations of monks and nuns recalled the passion of Christ in the most gruesome detail, and relics of the Crucifixion were eagerly sought after. In the presence of such close and visible evidence of death, the religious imagination worked overtime. The wound of the crucified Christ, which, according to the Gospel of John, was inflicted by a Roman soldier, became the access to the heart of Him who died for us. The fact that in Christian iconography the wound invariably shows up in the right side of the breast makes no difference; piety should not be confused with anatomy. Similarly, the French revolutionary Jean-Paul Marat did not escape death because Charlotte Corday stabbed him on the right. Many monks, nuns, and saints, including Catherine of Siena, worshiped the Sacred Heart of Christ, but this was a special cult at a rarefied level of mysticism and had no place in the devotions of ordinary people.

During the great religious controversies and conflicts of the sixteenth century, believers who had to make a personal choice between the old faith and the insurgent Reformation would speak of following the dictates of their heart. In addition to the Cross, Luther and Calvin included a heart in their seals and coats-of-arms. Their contemporary, Ignatius of Loyola, made sure that the escutcheon of his new Jesuit order not only depicted the nails with which Christ was crucified but also bore the image of the Sacred Heart. By the time of Harvey's work a century later, the heart had become the emblem of human transgression and divine redemption, and it was included, for ceremonial or poetic purposes, in coats-of-arms, in books of aphorisms, and in sermons and songs. The heart became a focal point of both anatomical research and religious exaltation, but in either case its appeal was to individuals. In his textbooks on human physiology written in the 1960s, psychiatrist J. H. Van den Berg beautifully delineates these two worlds and the bond between them—the heart as a mechanical pump and the heart as a divine source of life.

THE PUBLIC ADORATION of the Sacred Heart originated in the seventeenth century with the French nun Marguerite Marie Alacoque, one of countless forgotten saints who have served their purpose on earth and presumably in heaven. She lies in state in a shrine in the chapel of a Burgundian convent, her brain preserved in a heart-shaped reliquary. The chapel itself is a chaos of hearts of every shape and size, each aflame and bearing a cross. The overall effect is of unrestrained and unrefined religiosity, striking because of its almost insane monotony.

Marguerite Marie Alacoque, a notary's daughter, lost her father at an early age, suffered greatly at the hands of a malicious stepfather, and even at a very young age was unusually devout. As a child, she spent four years confined to her bed, in a state of skin and bones, but was cured by the Virgin Mary on condition that she enter a convent dedicated to the Virgin. This she did in 1671, when she was twenty-four, in Paray-le-Monial, a small town in the heart of Burgundy graced by a beautiful Romanesque church. One year later she made her vows and began to feel at one with Christ, a state of utter bliss after so much misery. While in the convent, she undoubtedly read the lives of the saints, in which veneration of the heart was an important feature, and probably knew of a contemporary cleric, Jean Eudes, who was exhorting town and countryside to worship the heart of the Mother of God.

Marguerite Marie mortified herself by doing the filthiest chores at the convent, and her dreams, full of self-doubt and guilt, made her physically ill. Those around her were uncertain for a time whether she was a saint or a witch, but they finally came to believe that Christ had made a miraculous appearance to her—that Christ had become her husband, she the ecstatic bride burning with love and desire, in a mystical marriage ceremony lasting three days and three nights. It was the high point of her humble and sickly life—the exchanging of her sinful heart for a celestial one.

Celestial, but flesh and blood, no longer just a symbol or emblem. She had many visions of Christ. In the first, a radiant Christ, through a wound in His chest, offers to impart His divine cardiac energy, and she is permitted to rest her head against His breast. He takes her heart, places it in His chest, and gives it back to her, sublimely charged. In the second vision, He displays the wound in His breast and, inside the wound, the burning heart that others cannot see or worship. When Christ appears for the third time, He again displays His heart, laments the rejection of His love, and asks for redress by the establishment of a feast day devoted to the Sacred Heart. About thirty such encounters follow, most of them involving the burning heart but rarely revealing the entire body of Christ.

The visions and the bleeding, burning heart at first aroused suspicion and mistrust in the convent. But that changed with the arrival of a new mother superior, and ultimately a chapel for the Sacred Heart was constructed. Marguerite Marie wrote about her visions and won over some Jesuits and other nuns. Emaciated but renowned, she died in her convent at the age of forty-three. The citizens of Paray-le-Monial anticipated events by already regarding her as a saint, and the Jesuit order undertook to promote the cult of the Sacred Heart, the Jesuits' tight organization, influence, and educational activity ensuring the cult's wide dissemination. It may be that Marguerite Marie also had practical feminine skills that began the tradition of the embroidered samplers, wall hangings, and other representations of the human heart we find today. I recommend the souvenir shop at the convent to any cardiologist who wishes to start such a collection.

The Church was not overly impressed by the new cult, although public veneration of the Sacred Heart spread like wildfire through France and was carried beyond its borders by missionaries. Then the Jesuits found the tide turned against them, as the rationalists of the Enlightenment argued against the worship of human organs. Some hundred years after the event, however, the Polish clergy asked the Vatican to sanction the adoration of the Sacred Heart, and it proved impossible for the Church to turn down this last wholly Catholic country. A decree approved the worship of the Sacred Heart and permitted a feast day and special mass devoted to it.

Thus the heart became the source of divine love. This heart was not Harvey's pump, not the seat of all-too-human emotions, and not a symbol; it was, rather, a physical sign of redemption, a direct mediator, exactly as the little nun had imagined. So the heart won a central place in both physiology and religion, and it would not yield that place for some time.

Other hearts were also being venerated, among them that of the Mother of God, a heart pure and full of maternal love. Indeed, Mary came to replace her Son in the religious culture. She materialized at Lourdes and performed miracles. In 1854, the pope proclaimed her Immaculate Conception as a step toward her deification. The beatification of Marguerite Marie did not occur until 1864. A trickle of pilgrims still visited Paray-le-Monial then, but France, on the way to *la belle époque*, was becoming a dechristianized country.

There followed the revolt of the Commune in Paris and the humiliating defeat of the Franco-Prussian War—God's punitive hand laid on the oldest daughter of the Church. The affluent bourgeoisie, in gratitude for having escaped both Karl Marx and the German kaiser, decided to erect a church of the Sacred Heart atop Montmartre, up to that time a refuge of artists and bohemians in one of the poorer quarters of Paris. The French state pledged the nation's support for the project, but forty years passed before the gigantic sugar-candy domes of the Sacré-Coeur were completed, on the eve of the First World War. The pope proclaimed the feast day of the Sacred Heart to have special significance for the Church, and a missionary society, the Apostolate of Prayer, spread the message of the Sacred Heart throughout the world, in many forms and languages.

In 1920, Marguerite Marie was promoted—canonized— whereupon hundreds of thousands began to flock to Paray-le-Monial every year. Popes and prelates visited the convent, and millions of Catholics joined prayer societies devoted to the Sacred Heart. Up to 1965, various encyclicals called for the veneration of the Sacred Heart, but then the cult started to wane. Only the current pope still seems to see something in it, but that may be because he comes from Poland. The veneration of the *human* heart had begun.

THE NINETEENTH-CENTURY adoration of the Sacred Heart had no counterpart in medical investigations of heart disease. In that time of high infant mortality and short life expectancy, heart diseases were much less common than infectious diseases (including tuberculosis) and accidents. The average person did not live long enough to reach the age of heart conditions, at least not of arteriosclerosis, the insidious vascular constriction that affects the heart, brain, and major arteries.

Of course, there had been occasional descriptions of symptoms encountered in clinical practice and in pathological anatomy. Around the middle of the nineteenth century, the famous Viennese pathologist Karl von Rokitansky described the thickening of the coronary arteries and correctly concluded that the deposits of fat, calcium, and fibrin came from the bloodstream—much as mineral deposits accumulate in water pipes. That this could lead to clinical complications remained unknown, however. Even Rokitansky's own final illness, involving angina pectoris and heart failure, was not diagnosed, either by him or by his physician; and, although he personally had performed sixty thousand autopsies, no postmortem examination was done on his own body. It wasn't until 1912 that a surgeon in Chicago, Dr. James Herrick, described the effects of an acute occlusion of a coronary artery by a thrombus, or blood clot. His was the first precise clinical picture of a heart attack.

In 1912 when Sacré-Coeur was nearing completion—the conception of the heart was much clearer to religion and sentiment than it was in the everyday practice of medicine. The stethoscope had been introduced, and doctors could hear the murmurs of leaking or occluded cardiac valves, but the electrocardiograph was not yet a feature of clinical practice, and it was barely possible even to measure blood pressure. One of the best-known surgeons in Europe, Dr. Albert Billroth of Vienna, said that anyone who attached importance to the heart deserved the scorn of his colleagues. Surgeons were terrified of operating on it, and it was virtually an unknown organ to the rest of medical science. Boston cardiologist Dr. Levine records in his textbook that during the First World War he diagnosed two cases of heart failure—a rarity, especially since, in his own words, Herrick's article had made no impression on him. Thomas Lewis, England's most prominent heart specialist between the two wars, devoted only seven pages of his 1940 textbook to the heart attack, which he said should be treated with morphine and strict bed rest.

After the Second World War, the heart attack came to be regarded as almost a judgment of God, which was being imposed with increasing frequency. It could strike anyone, especially men, without warning and with fatal effect. If the patient survived, he or she was put to bed and nursed, with hopes for the best but always in fear of a sudden end. With tuberculosis under control and the war over, this new and unexplained disease seemed to threaten even young men. American soldiers serving in the Korean War showed signs of arteriosclerosis at the age of twenty-two. Senator Lyndon B. Johnson and President Dwight D. Eisenhower suffered heart attacks in their mid-fifties, and the media followed the progress of their illness from day to day. No one was immune.

The experience gained in the epidemiology of tuberculosis now became useful in analyzing the causes of heart attacks. It turned out that there was a difference between East and West in the incidence of heart attacks. Three risk factors, the smoking of cigarettes, high blood pressure, and a high level of cholesterol in the blood, were found to increase the likelihood of an attack. One digs one's grave with a fork and a cigarette—our affluent life-style is also our downfall. Half of all deaths in the Western countries were caused by cardiac and vascular diseases, and of that number half were due to coronaries. The epidemic of guilt was followed by an epidemic of atonement: the pursuit of physical well-being through diet, jogging, weight-loss exercises, and abstinence. A new cult of the heart arose, which attempted to purge it of impurities by fasting and running. In America, smokers—who harm the environment as well as themselves —suffered outright discrimination, began to disappear from public life. The cholesterol chase was on. After 1972, the number of deaths attributable to heart attacks slowly, surely, and significantly declined in the West.

A new form of organ worship also took hold: if we could break our hearts, we would make them, too; after ruining them, we could heal them. Surgeons repaired or replaced diseased heart valves and constructed bypasses around constricted coronary arteries. Our life was prolonged by taking a detour: the surgeon holding a heart in his hands to repair it, while a heart-and-lung machine takes its place.

On December 3, 1967, it was shown that we could replace one person's diseased heart with the heart of another. That day, a little-known South African heart surgeon, Christiaan Barnard, disconnected the breathing apparatus connected to a black girl, a victim of a traffic accident. Her heart still beat, but she was no longer alive, because her brain was dead.

Science has learned that the heart is not the true nucleus of life, the first organ to become alive and the last to die. In the human embryo, the heart does not take form until the second month of pregnancy, and then it beats while the embryo develops. The heart is not the equivalent of human life—the aborting of a fetus no larger than three centimeters is sanctioned almost everywhere. What we have done is to shift the boundary at which life begins, but without defining life. At life's end we are more explicit. We have chosen brain death as the criterion.

The heart of the black girl was transplanted into the chest of a white recipient, Louis Washkansky (who would die later that month of an uncontrollable rejection reaction). Dr. Barnard became a media hero, and in 1968 other surgeons, in Texas, California, New York, Bombay, Paris, London, and Buenos Aires, tried to match his achievement, as though it were a sports contest. Most of the patients died within days or months because of their bodies' immunological response—a death rate as high as that of the hopeful ones on the waiting lists whose turn never came. The University Hospital of Boston decided against a heart-transplant program because, in the words of the philosopher Jeremy Bentham, it did not constitute the greatest benefit for the greatest number. But that reasoning didn't appeal to a world under the spell of the new medical miracle, no matter how few it was available to. Technology, which had proved so effective in space exploration, the information sciences, and nuclear energy, was also expected to help solve humanitarian and social problems. The surgeons waited for a better opportunity, and in 1980, when rejection could be more effectively controlled, a second round of activity began. Today, heart transplants have become standard treatment, with fully three-quarters of the patients surviving at least five years. Other techniques, involving the hearts of monkeys or artificial devices, have proved ineffective and inhumane. The heart once again becomes a symbol, one of giving and living. It appears on charity collection boxes and bumper stickers, in pop music and graffiti.

The success of heart transplants—the transformation of a mystical organ into a pump that can be replaced when it wears out—throws light on a related matter. Someone has to die first, someone young and healthy but with a dead brain, before the heart can be given. More heart patients are asking than there are donors available; many wait for a substitute heart that never comes. The cold facts indicate that with the growing demand, as life expectancy increases, half of all the candidates on the waiting list for heart transplants will die waiting. And thus the transplanted heart, like the Sacred Heart of Saint Marguerite Marie, again becomes a sign of grace, a gift given by one no longer living, who has chosen to bestow his life upon another.

The Neurotic Heart

THE TWO MEN, engaged in lively conversation as they strolled about Leiden on a sunny August afternoon, had much in common. The younger man, forty-five years old, sturdy, with a little blond fringe of a beard and hunched-up shoulders, moved at a brisk pace because he was used to long hikes in the mountains. The other, just turned fifty, slender and frail, with a high forehead and wearing spectacles, had a curious spasmodic gait. He, too, liked to hike in the mountains, though his doctors had advised him to take it easy, an admonition to which he paid little attention. Neither man was from Leiden; each was well known in his home city; and they were not acquainted. Both came from simple families, had made their names in their respective fields, and were accustomed to frequent and extensive travel, because of their professional activities and as a matter of personal choice. Both had recently visited the United States. The older man considered that country a mistake, the cuisine intolerable, and he didn't ever want to go there again, although it was where his achievements would meet with their greatest acceptance. The other had worked there for a few months on three separate occasions but had received little recognition from the Americans and would have to wait a long time before he did.

Both were recognized in the Netherlands, where they had good friends and where their innovative work was appreciated—partly due to the relaxed bourgeois-liberal atmosphere that then prevailed. Both men were Viennese Jews who in their life-style and work had abandoned tradition and orthodoxy. They had never met until this moment, and after their four-hour walk around Leiden they would never see each other again. They had an animated conversation, which both enjoyed, but it did not make a lasting impression on either man. What we know about this consultation of Gustav Mahler with Dr. Sigmund Freud, on August 26, 1910, is fragmentary, told long after the event and mostly at second hand.

Mahler had fled from Vienna; Freud would escape the city with great difficulty in 1938, after the German annexation, to die an exile in London a year later, of the mouth cancer that had plagued him for years. Nine months after the conversation in Leiden, Mahler returned to Vienna and died in that city, where he was celebrated not as a composer but as the conductor of the Vienna Opera, a snake pit of intrigues and considerable anti-Semitism.

Like Freud, Mahler hailed from one of the German-speaking crown lands in Moravia, a remote part of the Austro-Hungarian Empire, which had large Jewish communities. The year Mahler was born, Jews were granted permission to live and work elsewhere, and they began to emigrate to the cities, which offered greater opportunities. Mahler's family was an unhappy one. In Moravia, his father had worked his way up from small-time dealer to liquor merchant and married a young girl against her will, whom he treated tyrannically. Resigned to a life of drudgery, she brought fourteen children into the world. Six of them died in infancy of infectious diseases. But in those days half of all children died before they reached school age. The young Gustav proved to be a talented pianist, and his father realized that this ability would allow his son to go further than he ever had. The mother, exhausted by her pregnancies, the illnesses and deaths of her children, and domestic troubles and neglect, died young. The only picturesque aspects of young Gustav's life were the natural setting of mountains and valleys, the garrison in the little town, with its trumpets and parading soldiers, and the folk music of Moravia.

With the help of sponsors, the fifteen-year-old Mahler arrived in Vienna, the center of the empire's diverse political and cultural activities, to study music. He began to compose; he passed his final high-school examination. His first musical composition, however, failed to win praise from a jury, because Brahms, one of the judges, heard too much Wagner in it. Mahler became the bandmaster of various small orchestras at resorts frequented by the upper classes, but later conducted at the music theaters in Kassel, Prague, and Leipzig. These obligations left him little time for composing. His First Symphony, pervaded by the mysticism of nature, had a mixed reception because of its break with the music of Schubert and Bruckner. He became a conductor in the empire's second city, Budapest, where he overhauled the operatic repertoire; he did the same in Hamburg, in 1891. These were the *Wunderhorn* years, during which he reached maturity as a composer, wrote his first four symphonies, and earned the admiration of younger conductors, including Bruno Walter and Otto Klemperer.

In 1897, the position of conductor and leader of the court opera in Vienna fell vacant. Vienna, where the empire was singing its swan song amid the beauty and decay of the *fin de siècle*. Mahler got the appointment, but not until he was baptized a Catholic (the prerequisite for a court position), his conversion motivated by both career considerations and uncertain religious sentiments, for he was more a citizen of the world now than a Jew from the provinces. Like the poet Heinrich Heine, who had earlier called his baptismal certificate his ticket of admission to German culture, Mahler considered opera to be worth the baptism. His religion was his music, and he never entered a church again.

The Vienna Philharmonic was not only a symphony orchestra but also accompanied the performances of the Vienna Opera. Perfectionist, innovative, and completely dedicated, Mahler led the orchestra in both of these assignments. Only the summer months were left for his own work; the rest of the year, he was harnessed to a grueling schedule, bringing him both acclaim and criticism. Hugo Wolf, Brahms, Wagner, Bruckner, and Richard Strauss were his contemporaries, men among whom he hoped to find a place, and the musical scene of Vienna offered a great opportunity. But the price was high. The inner circle of Viennese culture around 1900 comprised composers Anton Webern and Arnold Schönberg, authors Robert Musil and Arthur Schnitzler, painters Gustav Klimt and Oskar Kokoschka, architects Adolf Loos and Otto Wagner, philosophers Ludwig Wittgenstein and Ernst Mach. Some were Jewish; they were accepted as artists but periodically attacked by anti-Semitic politicians and the press. The same phenomenon marked Mahler's coming to the Vienna Opera and his departure from it ten years later. Mahler himself showed no reaction, as if this had nothing to do with him. Theodor Herzl, on the other hand, who was in Mahler's class at school, was so hounded by anti-Semitism that he advocated the establishment of a Jewish state and published his famous book on the subject in the same year Mahler wrote his *Reformation* Symphony. As the music historian Norman Lebrecht writes, the one proclaimed national salvation and the other individual salvation. And yet Mahler knew neither Herzl nor Freud while he was in Vienna.

During his ten years with the Vienna Opera, Mahler became

a celebrity. He was recognized by coachmen, cheered by students, revered by artists. Rodin modeled a bust of him; Thomas Mann portrayed him as the tragic figure of Gustav Aschenbach in *Death in Venice*; Richard Strauss called himself the first Mahlerian. This was due to Mahler's perfectionism, evident from his approach to the performance of music and his regeneration of the music theater. The conducting of his own compositions took him away from Vienna. The prophet of a new kind of music did not have much of an audience in his own city.

Mahler was in his forties when, after a number of liaisons with singers, he finally met his muse. She was Alma Maria Schindler, the daughter of a painter; after her father's death, she had been taken into the family of the painter Carl Moll. Half Mahler's age, she was a woman of great beauty, intelligence, and musical talent. Following a brief romance, they were married in the Karlskirche in 1902 and spent their honeymoon on a concert trip to St. Petersburg. Alma was fond of her husband and recognized his genius, but the solitude Mahler needed for his composing, his performing obligations, and his day-to-day problems at the opera resulted in neglect, in mutual alienation followed by periods of reconciliation. Mahler loved his wife to distraction—when he was aware of her —but mostly he was obsessively immersed in his conducting and his composing.

About a hundred years earlier, in the same city of Vienna, during the last year of his life, Mozart wrote, as a gift for a friend who was a choirmaster, a motet forty-eight measures and two pages long, without making a single correction. This "Ave verum corpus," composed in haste, is great music filled with religious feeling. During the last year of Mahler's life, shortly after his conversation with Freud, he conducted his Eighth Symphony, an equally ravishing religious testament, the first part based on the old hymn "Veni creator spiritus," the second on Goethe's *Faust*. Mahler had started to work on the symphony in 1906. Willem Mengelberg, Mahler's champion in Amsterdam, received this first description of it in a letter: "All of nature finds its voice in it; it is my greatest achievement to date. Imagine the universe beginning to sound and resound." More than a thousand performers were called for, one hundred and seventy musicians and eight hundred and fifty singers, including three hundred and fifty children and eight soloists. The premiere took place on September 12, 1910, in Munich, at the opening of the new music hall. Schönberg, Klemperer, and Leopold Stokowski traveled to Munich for the occasion, as did Thomas Mann, Stefan Zweig, and Georges Clemenceau. Bruno Walter rehearsed the soloists.

It was the epitome of the romantic symphony, and the last of his own compositions that Mahler would conduct in Europe. His later works *Das Lied von der Erde* and the Ninth Symphony he never heard in performance, and the Tenth Symphony he never completed. The magnification of scale, to express the inexpressible, reached its limits in the Eighth Symphony. It was a triumph of creation, the realization of a dream, and its performance a happy moment in an unhappy life.

A series of disasters had struck Mahler in 1907. His work at the opera, in spite of the artistic triumphs, involved endless conflict. There were financial difficulties, bad reviews of his own compositions, depressing intrigues. Seeing no prospect of relief, Mahler decided to give up his position in Vienna. The Metropolitan Opera in New York offered a contract, and the New York Philharmonic wanted his leadership. Since his contract in New York would not take effect until the beginning of the following year, this would give him an opportunity to retreat to the Tyrol, far removed from all obligations, and spend time on his own work. Mahler handed in his resignation. With his wife and two daughters, he went off on vacation to the Austrian Tyrol.

Within three days the older child had contracted diphtheria. She became steadily worse, could hardly breathe from inflammation in her throat, and after two weeks an emergency operation was performed at the summer house and a tube inserted in her trachea. To no avail: the child died a day later, not yet five years old. The parents were as devastated as they were exhausted. Alma's mother, who had come to help, suffered a heart attack. The local doctor who was summoned to examine mother and daughter found that both women's hearts were under stress. He prescribed complete rest. At the time, cardiac insufficiency and strict rest were the standard diagnosis and therapy of the Viennese school for all forms of exhaustion and fatigue.

Mahler, half in jest, also asked to be examined. He was found to have a defective heart valve, possibly caused by the frequent throat infections he suffered. The doctor seemed sure of his diagnosis, and the two specialists Mahler consulted in Vienna confirmed it. Mahler was advised to avoid exertion and to give up mountain climbing, swimming, and long hikes. In his wife's biography, written thirty years later, he was depicted as an invalid. And he felt he was an invalid, but nevertheless traveled to St. Petersburg for the last of his European concert engagements. Then, fearing that his days were numbered but still wanting to live and do creative work, he set sail for New York.

Mahler's life there was no easier than it had been in Vienna. The Philharmonic and the Metropolitan Opera were both under the sway of matriarchies that regarded music only as an ornamental thing, interfered with programming and performances, and treated the conductor like a messenger boy. However, his contracts were for short periods of only a few months, and this left him time to compose. The result was a trilogy of leave-taking: the Ninth and the uncompleted Tenth symphonies, and *Das Lied von der Erde*, in which life and nature are once again experienced with great intensity as they are bid farewell, initially in protest, but finally in resignation.

Mahler's creative force was stronger than ever, but in body and mind he was a broken man. The loss of his young daughter had driven him further into the isolation of music, and he hardly noticed his wife. She continued to demand attention, complained of aches and pains, and went off to spas to seek a cure.

In the summer of 1910, while Mahler was absorbed in preparations for the debut of the Eighth Symphony and in the composition of the Tenth, Alma met and had an affair with the handsome young architect Walter Gropius, which she admitted to her husband. Alma had ambitions of her own; she, too, wanted to compose, and to lead a more active life—but Mahler didn't listen. Unhappy, frustrated, she reproached him for the inadequacy of their physical relations, for his impotence, for his indifference. But when Mahler told her to choose between him and Gropius, she stayed, young, beautiful, and frustrated but unable to leave this restless, introverted man.

The marital crisis aroused deep feelings of guilt in Mahler. To make amends, he dedicated the Eighth Symphony to Alma. He played the songs she had composed years before but which he could never be bothered to look at. He left little notes around the house telling her how much he needed and loved her. At the age of fifty, he found himself locked in a private hell of loneliness and self-recrimination. A neurologist acquaintance advised him to consult Freud. Mahler had been heard to tell friends that he had little confidence in any man who tried to analyze all problems from a single point of view. Nevertheless, he made an appointment with Freud, and then canceled it. He did this three times. But Freud was patient and said he was willing, even while on vacation in Noordwijk aan Zee, to meet with Mahler. At the end of August, without a word to any of his Dutch friends, Mahler took a train to Holland, en route sending forlorn love letters to Alma. On August 24 the long walk began from Huis ter Duin to Leiden.

At this point in Freud's life, his most important publications on psychoanalysis were behind him—his works on the interpretation of dreams, the role of sexuality, the psychopathology of daily existence—and he was enjoying a vacation at the seashore in Noordwijk aan Zee. He had shocked the bourgeoisie of Vienna by his identification of sexual experiences in childhood as the source of later neurotic disorders. Using his patients' dreams, word associations, and slips of the tongue, Freud had shown how to find the deep hidden origins of their neuroses. He had published detailed case histories to support his hypothesis that a person does not know himself, because his actions are determined by his subconscious. In spite of academic opposition, Freud had convinced such colleagues as Carl Jung and Alfred Adler of the truth of his insights, and his work had attracted attention abroad, where societies devoted to the study of his theories were being established.

He had not only applied his psychoanalytic insights to his patients in Vienna; he had also used them to throw light on history and civilization. In the summer of 1910, he completed an analysis of Leonardo da Vinci based in part on an early recollection he had found in Leonardo's notes. The memory involved a bird perched on Leonardo's cradle and touching his lips with its tail. The personality of Leonardo, the illegitimate child of a notary from Vinci, near Florence, could be explained by these few lines, Freud wrote. The bird was a vulture, which is the Egyptian symbol for the mother. Leonardo was raised without a father and was overly pampered by his abandoned mother. Later he and his mother were taken into the household of his father, who meanwhile had married someone of his own class. In Freud's interpretation, Leonardo, having acquired two mothers and a father who withdrew, saw himself as the Christ Child, cherished by the Virgin Mary and Saint Anne. This explained his homosexuality, the nature of his art, and his eventual preference for the natural sciences.

Although certain factual discrepancies were called to Freud's attention—for example, the vulture turned out to be a mistranslation of kite in Italian—he never retracted the analysis. He went to Paris after he left Noordwijk, to see Leonardo's self-portrait for himself. Freud was a stubborn man who did not like to have his conclusions questioned—a source of future friction between himself and his colleagues.

MAHLER AND FREUD strolled through Leiden, both explorers of new worlds and obsessed with their work. Both for this reason had neglected their wives, Mahler his lively and talented Alma, Freud his slovenly and shadowy Martha. What the two men had to say to each other about Mahler's marital problems was largely shaped by Freud's point of view. They were not kindred spirits: Mahler spoke to a man whose opinions he distrusted; Freud, to a fellow Viennese whose work he did not care for, because he had no ear for music. The encounter, then, may have made more of an impression on the admirers of the two men than it did on the men themselves. Immediately afterward, Mahler took the night train back to Munich, to begin rehearsals for the performance of the Eighth Symphony.

He wrote passionate letters to Alma, who had stayed in the Tyrol. In them, he declared that Freud was right, that she was the mainspring, the light of his life.

In 1933, Freud's pupil Theodore Reik fled to Holland to escape the Nazis. Like his mentor, he decided to write a psychobiography, this one of Mahler. Hearing about the meeting of Freud and Mahler in 1910, he wrote to Freud to ask about that conversation of almost a quarter century earlier. Freud, unsure of his dates, replied that on an afternoon in Leiden in 1912 or 1913 he had had an analytic session with Mahler, and had heard from others that it had proved beneficial. He indicated that in the course of the discussion the question had arisen of the conditions under which Mahler could love someone. Freud's psychological assessment of this brilliant man with whom he had talked for a few hours was that he was a compulsive neurotic fixated on his mother. These few lines in Freud's letter to Reik were for a long time the only available account of the meeting.

Then, in 1940, Alma Mahler published her memoirs. After Mahler's death, she became the wife, the muse, or the mistress of other geniuses—Bauhaus architect Gropius, painter Oskar Kokoschka, author Franz Werfel, dramatist Gerhart Hauptmann. She died in New York in 1964 at an advanced age. Looking back, Alma exaggerated many of her experiences. She wrote that Mahler realized that he was behaving like a neurotic, and that he revealed to Freud his strange frame of mind and his anxieties. Freud reportedly reprimanded him severely for attempting, in his condition, to bind a young woman to him. Freud, who knew Alma and her family, said that in Mahler she was seeing a father while Mahler, in Alma, was seeing a mother, a mother like his own, afflicted and careworn. The name of Mahler's mother was Marie, and from their first meeting Mahler sometimes called Alma by that name and expressed the wish that her face showed more signs of suffering. Alma also wrote that she had indeed always sought small, slender men who were wise and had inner strength, because that was the way she remembered her father and why she had loved him. She said that Freud's analysis reassured Mahler, although he refused to accept the mother-fixation idea because he didn't believe such things had any significance.

The fact is that none of the available correspondence indicates that Mahler ever called his wife anything but Alma or a diminutive of it. And, for all his ecstatic expressions of love, Mahler did not win her back. While he was rehearsing the Eighth Symphony in Munich, she was in a hotel with Gropius. The uncompleted sketches of the Tenth Symphony, on which Mahler had worked during the summer of 1908, are full of cries of despair directed at his wife. They are repetitions of the forlorn scribbles in the score of his Eighth Symphony: "*Für dich leben! Für dich sterben!*"

In the 1950s, the British music historian Donald Mitchell, who was working on a four-volume biography of Mahler and his music, asked the British psychoanalyst Ernest Jones if he could supply any further details about the consultation. Jones, who was not Jewish and did not speak German, had met Freud in 1908 and formed an enduring friendship with him. He promoted Freud's ideas in the English-speaking world. The year before the meeting in Leiden, he had accompanied Freud to America, and between 1953 and 1957 he completed the standard biography of Freud. But about the meeting between Mahler and Freud, Jones knew nothing.

What Jones did find in the archives was a letter from Freud to the French psychoanalyst Princess Marie Bonaparte, written in 1925. She was the person who in 1938 helped Freud escape from Nazi Vienna. This letter was never published in full, but a summary of it is included in the Jones biography, and Mitchell was permitted to see the letter. Jones and other admirers of Freud have made his correspondence public on a very selective basis, in order not to sully the master's image. But the fact that Freud was a man of flesh and blood—that he preferred his sister-in-law to his wife, had a temporary addiction to cocaine, despised such defectors as Adler, Tausk, and Jung, was a bad doctor on occasion, and failed to foresee the danger of Nazism—does not make him any less fascinating. Nor the fact that, like Mahler's, his marriage was a failure and his work took precedence over all else.

Freud's letter to Princess Bonaparte led Mitchell and Jones to revive the Alma-Marie motif—the interpretation based on Mahler's addressing his wife by his mother's name. (The other side of the coin is that Alma's foster father had been a painter, and maybe it was no coincidence that the husband in whom she was trying to find her father was named Mahler.) Freud believed that after the analysis Mahler overcame his impotence and the marriage was a happy one until his death. Mahler had also stated to Freud that he was constantly aware of his inability to attain perfection as a composer because his most sublime and noble passages, inspired by the most profound emotions, were always being ruined by the intrusion of ordinary melodies. His recollection of a quarrel between his parents when he was a child gave Freud the key. After the quarrel, Gustav left the house in despair as a street organ outside was playing the Viennese tune "*Ach, du lieber Augustin.*" From that time on, tragedy and banal entertainment were inextricably connected, in his mind and in his music. Mitchell cites a multitude of musical examples that illustrate this tension between the mundane and the sublime, the celebration of life and the resigned acceptance of death, cosmic violence and the street tune.

Mahler, having spoken about his troubled relationship with Alma and about the discord in his work, must have felt reassured when Freud brought order to the emotional confusion by directing him to his childhood. Perhaps that restored his self-confidence as a man and a husband. In her autobiography, Alma wrote that Freud raised the subconscious to the surface and forced it on the conscious—without the possibility of absolution such as the Catholic church offered. Mahler's confession may have brought him relief, she said, but it did not change him much. Psychotherapy was nothing but confession without pardon. Alma noted in her diary that she would play her part in the comedy to the end. Mahler's own supreme fulfillment as a creative artist came two weeks after Leiden, when the sounds of the Eighth Symphony rang out.

Gustav and Alma Mahler left for New York. There Mahler conducted his own and other contemporary compositions, which were received moderately well. He suffered from repeated throat infections accompanied by a high temperature. On February 21, 1911, he conducted despite a high fever and a sore throat. The sore throat went away, but the fever persisted, sometimes low, sometimes high; Mahler grew too weak to conduct, even though he continued making plans for performances. The former family doctor, Joseph Fraenkel, a Viennese immigrant, visited the Mahlers in their hotel. Fraenkel suspected that Mahler was suffering from bacterial endocarditis, an inflammation of the heart valves that at the time was fatal.

Its cause begins with the bacteria that constantly enter the bloodstream through minor lesions. In normal circumstances, they are quickly destroyed by the white corpuscles. But when the heart valves are malformed or have been damaged by disease, the bacteria become attached to the valves, where their attackers cannot get at them. They create new sources of infection through coagulation on the valves, which open and close less effectively; infected matter is also carried by the bloodstream to the brain, the skin, or the limbs. The infection can go undetected for weeks or months, but the disease ends in disorders of the heart, kidneys, and brain. It is diagnosed, today, by means of a bacterial culture taken from the patient's blood. Provided the illness is identified early and treated with strong doses of antibiotics, it is relatively easy to treat.

Believing that Mahler had this disease, which had been identified and described only a few years earlier, Fraenkel called in the eminent internist Dr. Emanuel Libman of Mount Sinai Hospital in New York. Libman had recently introduced blood cultures into clinical practice as a means of diagnosing fever, and had also provided a detailed picture of bacterial endocarditis. He and his assistant, a Dr. Baehr, discovered in Mahler the sounds typical of an impaired mitral valve, between the left breast and the left atrium, as well as the characteristic metastases of embolisms in the eyelids and skin deriving from the infected valves. The illness appeared to be well established. A vial of blood was taken for bacteriological examination, and four days later the diagnosis—the verdict—was confirmed: a streptococcal bacterium, originally from the pharynx, was multiplying in unmistakable colonies. The physicians told the patient their diagnosis and the unfavorable prognosis.

The patient had just one wish—to die in Vienna. Debilitated by fever and weight loss, he was nursed in his hotel by Alma and her mother, who had come from Vienna, as best they could. At the beginning of April, they all sailed for Europe. The liner's captain screened off a part of the sundeck for Mahler's use, but he had to be carried to it; his wife and mother-in-law tended him day and night. There was still hope of treatment in Paris, the center of bacteriological research, and upon his arrival in Cherbourg, on April 16, 1911, Mahler was conveyed to a hotel in Paris, where he seemed to feel better. He soon took a turn for the worse, however, and had to be hospitalized in Neuilly.

Mahler's last journey had attracted much public attention, and the press was closely following the course of his illness. A serum treatment in Paris had no effect, and so he was finally taken to Vienna on the Orient Express, to a sanatorium, where his condition steadily worsened. In his life and in his music, death had always been with him, from the funeral march in the First Symphony to the tremulous rhythms of the cellos in the first movement of the Ninth, with its slowly dying away conclusion, which represents, in Leonard Bernstein's view, the sounds of the composer's irregular heartbeat. Now Mahler sensed that death was imminent. Confused and emaciated, he called for Alma. He was given oxygen; compresses were placed on his inflamed knees. In his feverish dreams he moved his hands on the bedclothes, as if conducting, and sometimes he murmured Mozart's name. Toward the end he was given morphine, and after hours of gurgling caused by pulmonary edema he died, on the evening of May 18, 1911, during a thunderstorm, just as Beethoven had done. Mahler was buried near his daughter, under a simple gravestone carrying only his name. On May 23, his executor received a bill for 300 kronen (about $128) from Sigmund Freud "for a consultation of a number of hours in August 1910 in Leiden, to which I had proceeded at his request from Noordwijk aan Zee." Freud had seen Mahler's obituary in a newspaper.

The bill turned up at an auction in May 1985 at Sotheby's in London—offered in the same sale as a letter from Beethoven to his "*unsterbliche Geliebte*." It was because of Mahler's own undying but neglected beloved that he had sought out Freud, and that these two Viennese extremes, who left an indelible mark on music and on psychiatry, met briefly one summer afternoon in Leiden, barely understanding each other. The bill, its value increased a hundred times, was proof of the meeting. Apparently it had been paid in full.

Soldier's Heart

JULY 1, 1916, was a beautiful day in northern France. On that day there was to be an attempt to get the stalled war going again, and the British Expeditionary Force, under General Douglas Haig, was to lead the attack. The British would have support from their French allies, although the latter were still reeling from their enormous losses in the spring at the siege of Verdun. The attack was to follow the established pattern. A sustained artillery bombardment of the German positions along the rolling chalk hills north of the Somme would be succeeded by a frontal infantry attack along a twenty-five-mile stretch. The British army of 400,000, consisting mainly of newly arrived volunteers, was ready to fight but trained only in the tactic of charging with rifle and bayonet. The artillery, however, was supposed to pulverize the enemy with a bombardment of five days, and the rest would be a breeze.

The infernal noise of the cannon stopped, and a moment of silence fell at seven-thirty that morning. As soon as the ground attack began, the artillery was to redirect its fire farther to the German rear. Out of the trenches stormed soldiers, officers, buglers, Scotsmen in tartan kilts, through the barbed wire and across the no-man's-land toward the enemy. But the German troops, in impregnable trenches dug deep into the chalk, had survived the bombardment without significant damage. From the crest of their hills they cut down the soldiers with murderous machine-gun fire. One advancing line after another fell into barbed wire and shell holes like stalks of corn felled by a scythe. There was no lack of bravery; but, then, there was only one thing to do—continue the attack. Like the celebrated Light Brigade of the Crimean War, the men did not reason why; they followed their orders and died. At the end of the day, the British army had suffered 60,000 casualties; 20,000 killed, 40,000 wounded. And many of the wounded would die pitiful deaths. On this first day along the Somme, the British losses were greater than those of the Crimean War, the Anglo-Boer War, and the Korean War put together. When the battle ended at last, in November 1916, the Germans and the British had each lost almost 500,000 men and the French 200,000; an area of five miles had been retaken, but it was so devastated that after the Armistice the French government wanted to return it to woods because redeveloping it seemed pointless.

The battle of the Somme marked the end of the British soldiers' idealism. Belief in one's generals, in the justifications for the war, in victory—evaporated. The only loyalty left was that among fellow soldiers at the front, those human sacrifices on the fields of France and Flanders. After the Somme, another two million British casualties would be added, until exhaustion on both sides ended in Versailles. In the Somme valley alone there are fifty military cemeteries, the ultimate scars on the landscape. One soldier in ten did not survive the First World War.

Among the participants of the battle of the Somme was the English poet Siegfried Sassoon, a carefree member of the landed gentry who in the trenches encountered another world. He was wounded twice and received a distinguished citation for bravery. His war poems deal with the loss of life, the horror of war, the obtuseness of the generals. Back in England, recuperating, he refused to return to the front. He expected to be court-martialed, but since his doctors suspected that he might be suffering from shell shock, he was sent to a sanatorium. A man who did not want to fight had to be mentally unhinged. Sassoon felt guilty about leaving his comrades in the lurch, and so he returned to the front, was wounded a third time, and lived to see the end of the war, a captain and the war's official poet, whether he liked it or not.

There had at first been little outcry against the slaughter. Instances of cowardice or desertion were rare. Much patriotism and lust for adventure, followed by inertia and resignation. After Verdun and the Somme, however, and after a new French offensive in 1917 again cost tens of thousands of lives without accomplishing anything, the front-line troops began to protest. General Pétain, the defender of Verdun, was made commander in chief: he saved his troops from further useless assaults, saw that they got better food and shelter, and regained their confidence. He was one of the war's few military leaders to have witnessed with an aching heart the departure of raw recruits for Verdun, and their return, greatly reduced in number and broken in spirit. This endeared him to his subordinates and made him a marshal of France, a father figure in a desperate war—a role he tried to repeat, but with dire results, after the defeat of France in 1940.

Pétain and Sassoon both believed that the war could not be won by sacrificing people's lives and that peace would prove elusive without an attempt to reach a compromise. Verdun and the Somme had no strategic importance whatever; they were killing fields on which one side decided to bleed the other to death, no matter what the cost to itself. The disillusionment came later, when a whole generation failed to return from the battlefields.

For the soldiers in the trenches, there was no way out; all they could do was stick together. To be wounded might mean a trip home, but more often it meant being crippled or dead. Medical care was primitive and available only to the most gravely wounded. In the midst of so much death and destruction, infections, foot ailments, lice, and diarrhea hardly counted. Physical exhaustion resulting from lack of sleep, bad food, cold, rain, constant exposure to gunfire, and isolation led to a mental apathy that only the acutest peril could overcome. Trench warfare became a way of life, an acceptance of a fate that reduced the world to a small patch of dirt on the front line. There was no open resistance to this fate, but there was silent protest. Anxiety, seldom admitted, expressed itself in physical symptoms. Thousands were sent back behind the lines because of shell shock, a mental paralysis incurred during continuous artillery bombardment or combat. It was attributed to such physical factors as the changes in air pressure caused by explosions, which were said to result in brain damage or a defective supply of blood to the nerve cells. Shell shock could affect the most intrepid soldier, and a short leave was thought to be all he needed to make him fit again for battle.

Of the 360,000 men discharged from British military service on medical grounds, 40 percent were wounded. The second largest category, a tenth of the cases, involved a cardiac disorder, and fewer than 20,000 were discharged because of nervous complaints. Lung ailments caused by the cold or by poison gas, joint diseases, frostbite, and other afflictions accounted for the rest.

The cardiac disorder caused much concern. The origin of the syndrome was a mystery and its treatment problematic. The front line was no place for careful diagnostic procedures, and closer investigation appeared necessary. As early as 1915, the British Medical Research Council had recommended that research be undertaken; it requested that two hospitals, a total of 950 beds, be made available. The best doctors were assigned to the project, and they were joined by a number of American experts, all of them experienced clinicians or researchers in the field of cardiac disease. The work took place far from the front, and among all the specialists there was not one psychologist or psychiatrist or even an army doctor with combat experience.

The doctors at the front obviously had to keep their diagnoses uncomplicated, and they had little opportunity for the proper examination of cardiac disorders. One diagnosis they came up with was impaired heart function, or "soldier's heart." Another was valvular heart disease, when they could hear a murmur. Almost all complaints of fatigue, shortness of breath, palpitation, or giddiness were put into one of these two categories.

In British cardiology the heart was looked on as the taskmaster of circulation. Under stress, its muscle extended and contracted more vigorously. The heart muscle was the string of a bow; the pumped blood, the arrow, whose velocity increased the more the bow was bent. A failing heart was one that had lost its vigor as a result of external influences, not because of any structural defect in the organ itself.

William Harvey, the discoverer of the circulatory system, had prefaced his masterpiece on the function of the heart by comparing it to King Charles I, and to the sun; the heart was the sovereign of the body and the giver of life. The idea that the heart was not a master but a servant, subject to the other organs and controlled by a nervous system that could stimulate or restrain it, did not emerge until long after the First World War, and then not in England.

The English medical men were shrewd observers and described soldier's heart accurately, although they found it difficult to explain. One of the group, an American doctor named Levine, would later write that it cropped up in the most diverse circumstances. Sometimes during a soldier's first medical examination; more often in the field; but on occasion not until the man had been in the trenches for several years. Levine observed it more frequently in British troops than among American soldiers, because the British had been at war longer and had suffered greater fatigue. He attributed soldier's heart to the victim's constitution and the stress of war. Often the men with soldier's heart had previously suffered nervous disorders in civilian life, but there was not always such a history. The disorder rendered the men unfit for active service, and if they returned to the front after a leave, they almost always had to be sent home again. In Dr. Levine's opinion, a more thorough medical screening of military recruits would have saved some of these men from the affliction and its serious consequences.

His British colleague, James Mackenzie, the chairman of the research commission, in 1915 studied a group of 2,000 British soldiers suffering from soldier's heart. He identified such symptoms as physical exhaustion, fatigue, shortness of breath, clammy hands, depression, and anxiety. In 80 percent of the cases the ailment was preceded by an infection, and insufficient rest was almost invariably a factor.

A younger expert on the team was Thomas Lewis, a researcher and clinician who would dominate British cardiology between the two wars. An independent researcher, talented and tenacious, he began a systematic investigation of soldier's heart. The symptoms, he found, were similar to those experienced after great physical exertion, when the heart beats faster, blood pressure rises, and shortness of breath and dizziness occur. In his military patients, the slightest exertion was enough to induce them. Lewis was less interested in describing the syndrome than in relating it to the circumstance in which it occurred—that is, exertion. He wrote a monograph, "Soldier's Heart and the Effort Syndrome," for the information of doctors at the front. But the syndrome, he soon became aware, could be applied to an extremely heterogeneous range of patients. These included the physically weak and frail, but also healthy men who had experienced extreme fatigue on the front lines, and soldiers who had had serious infections or had suffered gas poisoning, and those with undetected heart ailments. In other words, there was a spectrum of causes leading to a single complaint: the inability to make a physical effort.

The patients were checked, X-rayed, and given electrocardiograms, but nothing concrete came to light. None of the available heart medicines brought any improvement. The only treatment that helped was a gradual and relaxed rehabilitation over a period of months. Half the patients were eventually able to make some degree of physical effort, but postexaminations in 1925 revealed that only one in seven had fully recovered; although in the other six no serious heart condition had developed. Dr. Lewis, like his mentor, Mackenzie, thought that an infection was the most likely cause, even if not directly. He and his group saw to it that the syndrome was acknowledged and veteran benefits awarded to those affected by it.

The American team was not convinced by the British conclusions, but it had joined the investigation later and had less experience of war. Infection and a susceptible constitution seemed to the Americans an inadequate explanation; they believed that the effort syndrome was a psychological condition brought on by anxiety and fear, that it would disappear when the source of stress was removed, or that it could be cured if treated as a neurosis.

The Americans were reminded of their Civil War, a foretaste of the First World War, with equally terrible battles, battles in which the two sides together lost half a million young men. Large numbers of Civil War soldiers in field hospitals had been found to suffer from fatigue, shortness of breath, and palpitation, a syndrome that was attributed to overexertion of the heart muscle. A British army doctor blamed the heavy backpacks (sometimes weighing a hundred pounds or more) and their coupling straps for interfering with circulation; and so the straps were altered. But the soundest analysis was advanced by a Philadelphia physician, Da Costa, who was attached to a military emergency hospital. He described a rapid pulse at rest, together with shortness of breath and disagreeable sensations in the region of the heart, often after a period of strenuous duty but sometimes present even before the soldier went into battle. Da Costa had also encountered this condition in otherwise apparently healthy civilians. It was a syndrome of unclear origin but clear clinical manifestations; incapacitating but not life threatening. He gave it the neutral name of "the vulnerable heart," and others would write about the "Da Costa syndrome." After the war it was renamed "neurocirculatory asthenia"—debility of the nervous and circulatory systems.

When the military doctors of the First World War resumed civilian practice, they began to find cases of soldier's heart in ordinary citizens, especially women far removed from the circumstances of war, infection, or the threat of death. An inventory of cases revealed that these women were usually about twenty-five and that among them the disorder was not uncommon. Emotional stress, large crowds, and exertion brought on the symptoms; reassurance and good care often caused them to disappear, although in some cases the patients resisted treatment. The syndrome recurred to some extent during the Second World War, and Lewis's successor, Dr. Paul Wood, concluded after extensive research that it was not the result of exhaustion, as his teacher had believed, but of anxiety. It was a reaction pattern linked to the neurotic personality. The effort syndrome wore battle dress; Wood's cardiac neurosis wore nylon stockings. Wood believed that women, Jews, and Italians, being more emotional than men, Englishmen, and Scotsmen, were more prone to suffer from the neurosis, and he was content to leave its treatment to psychiatrists and psychologists. These, unlike their cardiologist colleagues, held that the root of the effort syndrome lay in a fundamental personality defect resulting from early childhood conflicts.

A portrait of a man with soldier's heart, painted during the First World War, hangs in the museum of the Royal Postgraduate Medical School in London. It is a typical example of the disorder, and a reproduction of it appears in Dr. Wood's famous textbook on diseases of the heart. It shows a tall, thin man with a downcast and vacant gaze, slouched in an apathetic attitude, his large hands resting submissively on his knees. It is a picture eloquent of frailty, resignation, and fatigue.

Soldier's heart sprang from the war, no badge of courage but a symbol of infirmity of body and mind. It was the heart of those who could no longer endure the strain of war, a failing heart that was not the victor but the victim of the battlefield. Lieutenant-poet Siegfried Sassoon concludes his poem "Before Day," written in the year of the Somme, with these lines:

> For I am lone, a dweller among men,
> Hungered for what my heart shall never say.

———

Psychology has taught us that people respond to stress differently. A burden to one may be a challenge to another. War, famine, and oppression put pressure on an entire community, yet individuals come to terms with that pressure in widely divergent ways. It is a greater wonder that people returned from the trenches or from prison camps unbowed and sane, than that their lives afterward were scarred or ruined by the experience.

At the front and in the trenches, anxiety was pervasive, of course, but so was the denial of it; acceptance of fate or the instinct of self-preservation conquered fear. The deadening of all feeling was sometimes the price paid for survival. But fear and anxiety, suppressed, sought an acceptable outlet in fatigue, palpitations, and shortness of breath. Soldier's heart made the complainant unfit for service at the front, and that was more important than a precise diagnosis. The label gave the doctor and the army an honorable way to be rid of the unfit.

In my copy of Dr. Lewis's booklet on soldier's heart, someone has pasted in a few simple rules for the guidance of army doctors. A man unable to hop twenty times on one leg was suffering from an exertion syndrome. Infection, a susceptible constitution, poor nutrition, and a defective cardiac valve might be causes—cowardice, anxiety, or neurological disorder was not suspected, not assumed. American physicians later used the term "cardiac neurosis," but they also pointed out that the circumstances in which it occurred were unusual.

Under stress, the psyche may seek by physical manifestations to achieve mimesis: the imitation of one disorder by another. For example, the hysterical patients of Freud and Jean-Martin Charcot imitated the symptoms of neurological damage. To unmask a psychological mechanism of this nature was a great discovery. But heart disease was less prevalent in those days, and it occurred mostly in young people, whose heart valves malfunctioned as the result of rheumatic fever in childhood. Palpitation, a heart murmur, shortness of breath, and fatigue were the symptoms; the diagnosis was often just a lucky guess, and, as in Mahler's case, there was little to be done for the patient. Between the two world wars we find little mention of soldier's heart. Recruits of the Second World War received more thorough medical examinations, and many were rejected on mental grounds.

So this disease of the First World War did not outlive the Second. It had its day, as a sanctuary from anxiety, fatigue, or the inability to function, but there are now countless ways of examining the heart. Strictures of the coronary arteries are detected, arrhythmia—but no soldier's heart. The only connection still made today between heart disease and the psyche is an American one: the belief that a certain type of personality invites a heart attack. The man who is always in a hurry, always short of time, running until he drops. This type originated not on the banks of the Somme but along the Pacific coast of California, during the prosperous 1960s. It was behavior considered necessary to succeed in a white business world full of competition, aggression, and deadlines. But the personality type appears to be confined to one culture and one period—unexportable to Europe, at least, where it is not the managers but their subordinates who tend to get heart attacks. The fact is that although the world seems to be turning faster all the time and the demands on us keep increasing, the number of people dying of heart attacks is decreasing throughout the Western world, because today the heart is a pump that can be repaired.

PATHOLOGY, in medical science, is the ordering of clinical observations about a disease, usually made with the aid of measuring instruments. An illness is explained in terms of the biological mechanisms involved. Some illnesses are those mechanisms and nothing more, but there are illnesses that involve anxiety, pain, resistance, and hope. Deductive biological explanation has made a considerable contribution to medical science, but that does not turn medicine into applied biology. Even biological explanations are affected to some extent by subjective preferences, for example, the choice of measuring stick. Clinical practice at the beginning of the nineteenth century derived its knowledge of disease from the autopsy. The fact that most serious illnesses were fatal facilitated the early development of organ pathology, the scalpel revealing the cause of death. But death and the scalpel could not shed light on such functional disorders as high blood pressure, diabetes, or a defective thyroid. And infectious diseases could not be identified until their respective bacterial agents were discovered.

There is no hierarchy of diseases, such as the hierarchy of the natural world on which Linnaeus based his classification of plants. Rather, there is a constantly changing array of syndromes, sometimes of known but more often of hypothetical origin. Even when the cause is known and uncomplicated, the syndrome can resemble another in its symptoms, effects, and dynamics. The main purpose of classifying diseases is to indicate the treatment that should follow a given diagnosis. The classification is neither arbitrary nor objective, and diagnosis, as my Danish colleague Hulff puts it, remains a matter of personal opinion.

And these opinions change as diseases take new forms. Stomach ulcers and tuberculosis occur today, as they did a hundred years ago; but in a world that is radically different, they manifest themselves differently. In old age, which was reached by very few in earlier times, a disease has different characteristics than during middle age. Little wonder, then, that each era creates its own syndromes, classifications, and explanations. Freud and Charcot described hysteria, but their patients and their diagnoses belong to the world of yesterday and have little validity now.

Soldier's heart has disappeared along with the soldiers of Verdun and the Somme; it is only a memory, a faded label. We seem to know more; we have shortened our list of unexplained diseases; and soon we will be determining their causes on the basis of cells, through molecular biology. But a person is more than the total of his cells, tissues, and organs; his life, in the words of the famous anatomist Xavier Bichat (who used victims of the guillotine in his work), is a mustering of all his forces against impending death. Those forces are mental as well as physical, and from their call to arms new syndromes flow, which on occasion exhibit surprising similarities to the old. Soldier's heart has been succeeded by a new and related effort syndrome, again one of British origin.

It first appeared in 1955, in one of London's great university hospitals, when a small number of patients but hundreds of nurses began to complain of malaise, muscular weakness, and extreme fatigue—an effort syndrome so severe, some could not stand up. The complaints, especially those of fatigue and muscular weakness when making a physical effort, persisted in several cases for years. The specialists plied their trades: the virologist looked for a virus, the psychiatrist for hysteria, but no convincing evidence was found for either. The victims, suspected of malingering, were outraged; they formed a patients' union, which thousands of women, mostly young, joined. The majority of them had worked hard for years—as nurses, office workers, or in other service capacities—and were still not recovered from the disease, whether it was infectious or not. They believed it was viral, like shingles or certain inflammations of the liver, and that it was located in the brain and muscles—a chronic myalgic encephalitis. Some patients were found to have antibodies against typhoid fever, and others exhibited defective stimulus responses of the leg muscles, but the findings were inconclusive.

The indecision of the various specialists fed the victims' suspicions that they were being discriminated against, and their union became more militant—jobs, termination pay, and recognition of disability status were involved. They mobilized some medical support for their claims; but sustained and thorough research, using every new technology, failed to find a virus or any cranial or muscular infection—although the data did not rule them out, either.

Chronic myalgic encephalitis had such an unmistakable pathological profile in England that it came to be called by its initials, CME (as many diseases are today, like AIDS). The disorder runs the same course as soldier's heart, is a chronic inability to exert physical effort due to tired muscles and dizziness, and often follows an infection, to which it was initially attributed by physicians, as Lewis and Mackenzie had done seventy years before.

But anyone today who suggests the possibility of a neurosis can expect a cry of indignation from the numerous CME sufferers and their supporters, in England and elsewhere. This activism has hindered a sensible approach to the syndrome, the cause of which continues to escape us—but in which, as in soldier's heart, psychology plays a major role. To reject this militates against the identification of the disease and its eventual treatment.

In their distress, people who are unwell often describe their ailment in a fanciful way, not able to find the words that a doctor can understand. This happens with any ailment, whether of the heart, the head, the back, or the stomach. One example cited by an old intestinal surgeon in Berlin, back in 1900, was that the duodenum, too, can weep. The soldier's heart muscle and the nurse's leg muscles have reasons medical science knows nothing of (or does not wish to). A symptom can be read only by one who is willing to read it.

Extremes of Men and Knives

The Perfect Crime

THE STAB WAS PERFECT. The weapon, a simple French kitchen knife with a wooden handle, had an eight-inch blade, long enough to penetrate deeply into the chest. The point entered between the upper ribs on the right side, near the breastbone, to the left and down. It perforated the right lung and the pulmonary artery, grazed the atrial auricle, and, finally, severed the aorta, close to the heart.

The massive bleeding was fatal within seconds. The victim had time to utter only one scream for help; it was heard in the warm summer evening by the neighbors at their open windows. The victim's mistress and a neighbor who was a doctor tried to stem the gushing flow of blood, but it was too late. The conditions were right for the blow to be mortal. The victim was slight of build, naked, and sitting up in the bathtub. The stabber, standing over him, was able to plunge the knife in with full force. The autopsy the next morning revealed the fatal rupture of the major blood vessels of the chest.

It was a premeditated murder, but also a murder of passion; flawlessly executed, but by an unpracticed female hand. She knew the victim only by name, but the name was that of a monster—though some considered him a public benefactor. Charlotte Corday, a maiden, was the executioner of executioner Jean-Paul Marat. After that warm summer evening of July 13, 1793, she would pass into history, her name forever linked to his.

There is little to relate about the life of Charlotte Corday. She died under the guillotine at the age of twenty-five, after an uneventful country existence in Normandy that culminated in her one trip to the capital city of Paris. Descended from rural aristocracy, she grew up in respectable poverty, first on the family farm near Caen and later in the town. There, in shabby quarters, her mother and her eldest sister died, and at fifteen Charlotte had to assume responsibility for the family. She attended a convent school for girls from good homes but without means. There she read the classics, including Rousseau and her distant forefather Corneille; did good works; received a religious education. From what we know, she was sturdy, healthy, and attractive, with an open, fresh face, a fair complexion, and auburn hair.

In 1789, the year the French Revolution began, Charlotte Corday decided to become a nun. The Third Estate had withdrawn from the States-General, broken with the Church and the aristocracy, and created the National Assembly to draw up a constitution for France. In these circumstances, however, becoming a nun did not seem inappropriate; the Declaration of the Rights of Man, promulgated in August 1789, guaranteed freedom of religion.

But the National Assembly soon split into irreconcilable factions. The Revolution began to seem permanent, going from bad to worse and culminating in the Terror, until finally, in July 1794, the last head, that of Robespierre, rolled from the guillotine. As early as the summer of 1789 there was unrest and anarchy in the streets, and not just in Paris. In Caen, a mob lynched an arrogant lieutenant of a royal regiment, tore his heart from his chest, and hacked off his head and carried it on a stake to show to the abbess.

The king and queen were being held captive in the Tuileries, the aristocracy was abolished, and the possessions of the Church were confiscated. The radical Jacobins grabbed power throughout the country, suppressing the more moderate Girondists. The virtual extinction of the Girondists by Marat in June 1793 would mark the beginning of the Terror, shortly before Marat's own demise. Famine and want were widespread, and an unsuccessful war was being waged on the frontiers.

In 1791 the religious houses were outlawed. Charlotte Corday returned to her father's farm and later moved in with an elderly aunt, to serve as her companion and lead the life of a spinster. Events in Paris were the subject of heated discussions, and, according to her contemporaries, Charlotte was said to have expressed sympathy for the Girondists and their moderate policies. Caen, two days' journey from Paris, experienced little of the violence that was taking place elsewhere, although violence was anticipated.

A coalition of foreign foes was threatening to march on Paris if any harm came to the king, now a prisoner in the Temple. The National Convention was beset by internal wrangling, and in the absence of strong leadership the power vacuum was filled by the Paris Commune. Inspired by Marat, this was a municipal body bent on settling accounts, with the assistance of hired thugs from the slums of the south, mainly Marseilles. The passionate flag-waving song they sang, composed a few years earlier by a young ensign in the French army, progressed triumphally from the gutter to the status of national anthem. The composer's mother was ashamed of his "Marseillaise," and the ensign himself ended up in prison.

Marat, a journalist whose writings embodied the fury of the people, could now put into practice what he had preached for years. Hired gangs carried out a preconceived plan to arrest and murder some three or four thousand of Marat's opponents.

A Committee of Public Safety drew up lists of victims—the clergy, the aristocracy, and ordinary citizens—and systematically seized their property. Mobs stormed the prisons, and their massacres took the lives of 1,500 men, women, and children. The September killings of 1792 went on for a week. Power was in the hands of an unholy trinity of Marat, Danton, and Robespierre, who were themselves destined to be destroyed by the violence they had unleashed. The trial of the king followed, in December 1792, and his execution on January 21, 1793. Louis XVI may have been a weak king, but he was not hated and was not a tyrant, and his execution divided the French people forever. One can condemn a monarchy without decapitating its king.

The weakened Girondists, trying to impeach Marat, were in consequence expelled from the National Convention. They then sought support in the provinces against the Parisian Reign of Terror, which they felt was betraying the Revolution for the sake of power. In Normandy also the Girondists were mustering troops to march on Paris and put an end to the Jacobin coup.

It must have been during that spring of 1793 that Charlotte Corday decided to do something—to murder the very symbol of the bloodthirstiness, Marat, preferably in public, in the meeting hall of the National Convention. On the pretext of having to plead a friend's case for a pension, she traveled to Paris by coach, checked into a modest hotel, addressed a letter to the people of France, and put the letter in her bodice, along with a knife she had picked up somewhere.

Marat lived where the huge premises of the Faculty of Paris are now located, in the Cordeliers district, an ancient quarter on the Left Bank. He lived on the second floor of an apartment building on a narrow street; it was reached by means of a stone staircase. The premises were luxurious, consisting of seven rooms with open fireplaces and marble floors, but dirty and neglected by the occupants, Marat, his mistress, and two female relatives. On the fatal Saturday, July 13, Charlotte Corday came to the door three times and asked to be allowed inside to report on a Girondist plot in Caen. Toward evening she was finally admitted. She was well dressed, had had her hair done, and wore a black hat with green ribbons, which figures in all subsequent depictions of the event. Marat was sitting in his bathtub working on articles for his newspaper. It was his habit to receive visitors this way—he was afflicted by ailments of the skin and joints, and the bath gave him some relief. Visitors sat on a stool alongside to converse with him.

Charlotte Corday's interview with Jean-Paul Marat did not last long. She told him about the revolt in Caen, and he asked for the names of the Girondists, so that he could dispatch them to the guillotine as soon as possible—a prospect he obviously relished. He took down their names, put his pen on a small chest next to the tub, and then must have felt the knife.

Marat's death was neither unexpected nor undeserved— he was the Joseph Goebbels of his day. A cultivated man with a good education and considerable linguistic ability, he had written many books on the natural sciences. But his aspirations were crushed when he failed to gain admission to any scientific association. A fanatical student of all the sciences, he wandered through Europe, lived for a time in England and the Netherlands, and graduated as a doctor of medicine in Scotland. After all this roaming, he returned to France and entered the employ of the king's brother, the Count of Artois, and began a reasonably successful medical practice. He was more interested in research, however, than in his patients. But his scientific efforts went unappreciated in every quarter, and gradually he developed an obsessive hatred for everyone who had denied him recognition. He lost his position and his practice, neglected himself, thirsted for blood. The Revolution finally gave him the opportunity to distinguish himself, but even then he continued to make enemies by his almost demonic hatred and need for vengeance. A loner, often despised and mocked, he belonged to no political group or party and was contemptuous of everyone. He was small, ugly, and disfigured by a scaly skin disease, probably advanced psoriasis or herpes. Gruff in manner and badly dressed, he inspired fear rather than respect. He lived hidden in a maze of medieval streets and alleys, surrounded by other revolutionaries, often on the run, a mystery to his opponents. His loyal mistress, Simone Evrard, looked after his home, giving him a private place to withdraw to, and took care of him without sharing his political ambitions. Marat's fidelity to Simone—his last cry was for her—is the only human sentiment ever detected in him.

He began to make his reputation with the founding of his newspaper, *L'Ami du Peuple*, which called itself the avenue to freedom; it exhorted action, vengeance, and bloodletting, in an endless series of articles that turned out to be self-fulfilling prophecies. This made him known, feared, and hated throughout France. When the Paris Commune, through the Committee of Public Safety, loosed the mob on its enemies, Marat replaced his pen with terror. His death in his bath, in the midst of all the frightfulness and bloodshed in the streets, was nevertheless a shocking event. More than once, verbally and in writing, Marat had offered himself as a martyr, and he openly carried a pistol, swearing he would shoot himself in the head if ever challenged by the Girondists. A nihilist, he was familiar with indiscriminate violence and knew he might himself become its victim. But that he should be struck down on a Saturday evening in his bath by a God-fearing convent girl from distant Caen surprised everyone. The various opinions, put forth at the time and years later, are of interest because of ways in which the event was distorted.

Marat's death became known in Paris the following day, but the lack of information led to rumors of all kinds. The National Convention immediately memorialized him as a martyr, and the famous painter of the Revolution, Jacques-Louis David, was commissioned to depict the death scene. The painter had visited Marat the day before his murder and had also found him sitting in his bathtub and writing in the interests of the people. That was how David wished to paint him, but first the body had to be prepared for the lying in state. The same physician who had performed the autopsy in the morning began the embalming on Sunday afternoon. The heart was saved so it could be displayed in an urn in Marat's Club des Cordeliers; the intestines were removed; the wound, encrusted with blood, was left undisturbed. The doctor, named Deschamps, and his five assistants went to a great deal of trouble and charged the huge sum of 5,000 livres—which the municipality of Paris beat down to 1,500 livres. The lying in state was held in the Church of the Cordeliers, which had been desecrated by the Revolution and whose monastery had become a lodging for extremists of all descriptions. The deceased was laid on a triumphal bed decorated with the French tricolor, his body half covered by a sheet. The part of the torso with the bloody wound was left exposed. The bed was strewn with flowers, and a wreath of oak leaves hung above his head. The bathtub and the bloodstained knife were displayed below the bier. His last newspaper columns had been reprinted and were available in the chapels. The steps of the altar bore the inscription "Marat, friend of the Nation. Enemies of the Nation, temper your joy, for there will be avengers!"

The intention was for the body to remain on display for some days and then be taken on a journey throughout France. But nature prevailed over the Revolution's new gospel. In the warm summer weather, blemishes appeared on the body, and it began to smell—the reason the bier was raised so high and was regularly sprinkled with herbs and rosewater. The ceremonial proceedings became a rather lugubrious affair, and it was decided to bury Marat on Tuesday, in the garden of the monastery, where he had conducted political classes. The funeral procession moved through the *arrondissements* of Paris from six in the evening until after midnight, followed by a motley crowd, with music, flags, torches, and the firing of cannons. The corpse, turning green and giving off a strong odor, was borne along on its triumphal bier, and people threw flowers on it. After some speeches in the monastery garden, oaths were taken that Marat's murderous work would be carried on. A second, more modest service was held a few days later in the Club des Cordeliers, where his heart would remain. It was preserved in a beautiful urn of royal provenance, the lid encrusted with precious stones.

If Marat eventually came to be thought of as a mangy hyena, the murderess was the picture of rosy innocence, a sturdy lass from the country. She did not try to run away, but calmly accepted the consequences of her deed, knowing what they would be and quite prepared for them. After her arrest, she said she had feared that Marat was inciting civil war and that she had come to Paris to kill him and sacrifice her life for her country. At her preliminary hearing she was calm and dignified, losing her composure only when she had to view Marat's body and listen to the uncontrolled sobbing of Simone

Evrard—proof that someone had cared for him. Corday was taken to prison to await her trial before the brand-new Revolutionary Tribunal, whose notorious public prosecutor, Antoine Fouquier-Tinville, was hoping to uncover a plot. The trial, the day after Marat's spectacular funeral, was another public entertainment. Corday maintained that by her act she had brought peace to her country, that she had slain one man to save hundreds of thousands. To this end, she was happy to offer her life. A plea of insanity was suggested to her lawyer, but he decided against it, in view of her supreme tranquillity and composure and the absence of any signs of remorse. At the end of the morning the sentence of death was passed, and the same afternoon it was carried out at the guillotine. There was little justice in the proceedings, but they did have the merit of brevity.

Charlotte Corday's final hours were spent posing for a portrait and having her long curls cut off to expose her neck to the blade. She donned the red shirt that murderers were obliged to wear and, with her hands tied behind her back, was conveyed in a cart to the Place de la Concorde. Standing erect, drenched by a sudden downpour, young, pretty, and self-assured, she went to her death. She was tied to a board and placed under the blade, which seconds later severed her head from her body. An assistant executioner held up the head for the crowd to see and slapped the cheeks, which were alleged to blush. For this unworthy action, the assistant was reprimanded by his chief, Charles Sanson, a member of a dynasty of executioners who had begun their careers under Louis XIV and would not give them up until 1848, for lack of employment.

Sanson was an officer of the new republic and a purveyor of equality via the guillotine. In March 1792, he had complained to the minister of justice that an official execution by decapitation with a sword required both a skilled executioner and a brave victim, and that there were more condemned than swords in Paris. Sanson requested a better method of carrying out the National Assembly's intentions. A method was suggested by a philanthropic doctor and member of the assembly, Henri Guillotin, who argued for equal punishment for equal crimes, carried out in a uniform manner by means of a simple machine. Until that time, aristocrats had been decapitated by the sword, ordinary citizens hanged, and regicides drawn and quartered. A single, simple, mechanical procedure for all condemned persons would be more humane and democratic. The falling ax had appeared in a few other countries. Given the uncertain swordsmanship of the Sanson family, along with the fear that common citizens would go to their deaths less resolutely than aristocrats, it might be a preferable method of execution.

The German carpenter who built the device hoped, by patenting it, to sell this tangible product of the Enlightenment to many French cities. Even before its inauguration in April 1792, it was the subject of an engraving in which decapitation was depicted as a sacred ceremony: the populace was kept at a distance, the victim had a last word with the father confessor, and the executioner bowed his head as he cut the rope that kept the blade aloft—all this set in a lovely landscape. The real thing was another matter, applied on a much larger scale and more barbarously, yet it was consistent with the ideal that the administration of justice should be equal, humane, public, and impartial, whether the victim was a king, a criminal, or a girl named Charlotte Corday. The posthumous insult to Corday by the executioner's assistant broke an unwritten rule of the theater of the Revolution, and people interpreted the blush on the cheeks of the head as a supernatural reproach.

To the masses the mechanical death may have been a common spectacle, but the physicians who had pleaded for the device were fascinated by the question of whether the soul or personality lingered a moment in the severed head. The well-known physiologist Xavier Bichat, intrigued by the fault line between life and death, sometimes stood beside the scaffold, ready to test whether the heart could still be stimulated by an electric impulse. Some physicians shouted into the ears of the heads to see if there was any visible reaction. Others pressed the separated heads and bodies together and claimed to detect signs of life. But they all finally had to settle for the rule that young military doctors would be taught in the 1950s: death has occurred when the head and body are separated.

Even after her death, Corday did not escape the medical profession. An autopsy was performed in a nearby hospital, under the supervision of a government commission headed by the omnipresent David, and she proved to have been a virgin. Her body was placed in a mass grave behind the Madeleine. Her head remained unburied; the skull reportedly ended up in the possession of Princess Marie Bonaparte, whom we met in a previous chapter.

Charlotte Corday, as she wrote in a letter shortly before her execution, judged her life in terms of its usefulness. She had hoped, by her deed, to prevent the violence of a civil war. But her family considered her a murderess and never mentioned her name again. After her death, the Terror erupted in its full and appalling force and claimed hundreds of thousands of more lives.

MEANWHILE, the memorializing of Marat was assuming gigantic proportions. Streets and squares were renamed for him; portraits and busts appeared; his bathtub and his papers were put on display. The death scene was reenacted in songs, plays, and drawings. Children were baptized Marat. People crossed themselves as they uttered his name. In Sèvres his image was baked in porcelain. Marat, the people's martyr, acquired in death a glory he had been unable to achieve during his life. The National Convention decided to reward his martyrdom with apotheosis, the epitome of honors: the privilege of lying in the Pantheon. Under royal patronage, this old church had been converted into a classical temple to serve as a resting place for the heroes of Liberty. The remains of Voltaire, Mirabeau, and Rousseau were there; Marat would lie with them.

But Marat owes his immortality in part to another. The artist David (who directed Marat's funeral) had done a painting that would make both himself and Marat famous. He depicted the dead revolutionary in his bath, goose-quill pen and paper still in his hands. The note from Corday asking his benevolent assistance rests on the little chest he used as a desk beside the bath. Marat is leaning against a white sheet, and the stab wound is clearly visible. The painting has more than one meaning. It is a masterful political portrait that immediately aroused great emotion; but it is also a classical image of human sacrifice, a *pietà* of the Revolution. The note Marat holds in his hand is a bequest of money to a widow with five children whose husband has fallen in the service of the fatherland. Everywhere there is blood, on the sheet and on the papers, and we see the knife lying on the floor. The dead Christ has become the dead Marat. The one thing that could have spoiled his appearance, his skin disease, is omitted. And the kitchen knife has acquired an ivory handle.

Art critic Kenneth Clark writes that all totalitarian art must of necessity be in the classical style. The state requires an art based on submission, not on the rebellion of the romantic

individualist. Classical art—clear, unambiguous, realistic, designed to inspire veneration—exactly fills the bill. David produced a work of art intended to hang forever in the
Convention's meeting hall. Thousands of engravings were to
be made of it; a Gobelin tapestry copy was to be woven. None
of this happened, and a few years later the painting was returned to the artist. After the Revolution—in the course of
which David himself landed in prison—he offered his services
to the Emperor Napoleon, whom he painted as Hannibal cross-
ing the Alps. When the monarchy was restored, David was
banished to Brussels—there was no place in France for the
"court painter" of the Revolution and the Empire. His widow
sold his works, and the painting of Marat now hangs in the
Palace of Fine Arts in Brussels.

Marat's apotheosis took place on September 21, 1794, a
Revolutionary holiday. An official of the National Convention
knocked at the doors of the Pantheon and in a loud voice read
the decree that invested Marat with the crown of immortality.
To the accompaniment of a choir, the coffin was put in place
and speeches delivered. A song in praise of the martyr of liberty,
music by Cherubini, concluded the ceremony. While the remains of the most recent hero of the Revolution were being
laid to rest, those of the first hero, Mirabeau, who had defended
the Third Estate against the royal troops, were being taken
out. Marat himself had not cared much for the hero worship
the republic had initiated, although he conceded that the republic needed founding fathers whom the people could
support.

Barely three years later, after the Terror ended, the National Convention decided that no one who had been dead
less than ten years should be buried in the Pantheon. In a
number of theaters, busts of Marat were removed from their

pedestals, and an effigy of him was burned in public and the ashes carried through the streets in a chamber pot. In February 1795, Marat's coffin was taken from the Pantheon and reburied in the nearest cemetery, which was razed at the beginning of the nineteenth century to make space for an electric power station. Medical expert Auguste Cabanes, who around 1900 made many medical-historical observations about the Revolution, thought that the station was an appropriate resting place for Marat, who as a student of science and doctor had written books on electrotherapy.

But that is not quite the end of the story. In 1889, it came out that Marat's bathtub now belonged to a clergyman in Brittany, who was putting it up for auction. A waxworks gallery in Paris, recently established by a Madame Grévin, outbid Madame Tussaud's museum in London. Which was only fair: Tussaud, learning her trade in Paris from her uncle, a doctor named Curtius, had made many death masks of heads that had fallen under the guillotine. She and her uncle probably assisted David by fashioning a wax model on which he could base his famous painting of Marat. When the Revolution ended, she departed for London with her collection.

The Pantheon, formerly the Church of Sainte Geneviève, the patron saint of Paris, is virtually empty. The saint's remains were disinterred and burned in public, and her sarcophagus is vacant. Pascal and Racine are still buried there, and in 1885 Victor Hugo was given a place. The last upheaval in the building occurred in 1870, when for a short time it was the headquarters of the Paris Commune.

Simone Evrard, Marat's mistress (known after his death as the widow Marat), lived on quietly; she died at the age of sixty, after a fall. Marat's sister, Albertine, who lived with him at the time of the murder, preserved the legacy of the martyr for liberty by turning her rooms into a museum. As a witness of the event and the conservator of her brother's papers, she was consulted by authors and historians. She died in 1841, at the age of eighty-three, having already passed on some of the legacy to visitors. One of them, a Colonel Maurin, an avid collector of souvenirs of the Revolution, received a few blood-stained pages of *L'Ami du Peuple*, Marat's newspaper, as a gift. The pages supposedly had been lying on the little chest beside the bathtub when the stabbing occurred. On the colonel's death, they were inherited by a count, who didn't want the grisly items and gave them for safekeeping to the father of the author Anatole France, who ultimately became the owner.

These pages reappeared in 1900, when they were displayed at the World Exhibition in Paris, along with a bound volume of Marat's work that contained eight other bloodstained news-paper pages. The volume had been purchased at a bookstall along the Seine, wrapped in brown paper on which was a note, in Albertine's handwriting, that these were some of Marat's papers that had been lying on the little chest beside the bathtub when he was murdered. According to Auguste Cabanes, both sections of newspaper were dated the thirteenth—but of June, 1793, not the fatal thirteenth of July.

MARAT AND CORDAY, dead for almost two centuries, are practically forgotten today. On occasion they are taken out of the mothballs of history to support some argument or other. Depending on the individual point of view, Marat is either the Christ of the rejected of this earth or a rat from the sewers of Paris; and Corday, either a second Joan of Arc trying to save France or a fanatical murderess. Had he lived, Marat would probably not have escaped the guillotine—his brothers-in-arms Danton and Robespierre did not. In the end, the French Revolution devoured its own children. It was followed by the Russian and the Chinese revolutions, each with its own heroes, men worshiped as Marat had been, but ultimately reviled because their blood lust cost millions of lives, fertilizer for the fields of the future, because the dream of equality was realized not in freedom but through force.

Marat was prepared, in word and deed, to let thousands perish; his pen, its power magnified a thousandfold by the printing press, was his weapon. *L'Ami du Peuple* was the embodiment of the fury of the people. Yet Marat did not die on the barricades but in his bath, and not by a sword but by a kitchen knife, his goose-quill pen in his hand. The murderous writer was murdered beside his desk, his blood on his newspaper but not on his hands.

The real enigma of the thirteenth of July remains Charlotte Corday, of whom we know so little except for the last week of her life. She sacrificed her life by killing a tyrant. It were better, as the high priest Caiaphas said to the Jewish council that condemned Christ, that one man die for the people than that the whole people perish. The death of Marat would be the price for the liberty of France, and Corday regarded herself as no more than the instrument to this end. It makes little difference that her deed did not achieve its goal. She made her sacrifice gladly, just as she had sacrificed her youth to her family and her adulthood to the convent. Some consider that it was two fanatics who encountered each other at the bathtub in the Rue des Cordeliers on a warm summer evening before the onset of the great Terror—a man demanding two hundred thousand heads in a public cause and a woman bent on destroying one who symbolized destruction in her native land. They were opposites, each prepared to go to the limit. The result was a perfect crime, a turning point in the course of the French Revolution.

The Anatomy Lesson

DEATH HAS MANY ASPECTS, in the past as well as today. A survey of how death has been depicted in sculpture and painting through the ages would cast an instructive if somewhat macabre light on the changing view of mortality in Western society. The Dutch golden age of the seventeenth century produced one of the characteristic representations, in the form of a painting of an anatomy lesson. From it we learn little about the dead man, but a great deal about those looking on.

Rembrandt painted his celebrated *Anatomy Lesson of Dr. Nicolaas Tulp* early in his career as a portrait painter in Amsterdam. In that year, 1632, knowledge of anatomy as studied with the naked eye had progressed as far as it could. Four years earlier, the Englishman William Harvey had described the circulation of the blood. As for Tulp, his fame as an anatomist would soon be eclipsed by the work of the lensmaker Antonie van Leeuwenhoek, born in Delft that same year, whose microscope would make the invisible visible. The structure of the dead body was known; it was how the living body functioned that would become the new field for study.

The most interesting thing about the *Anatomy Lesson* is the glimpse it gives of certain medical and administrative aspects of death in the flourishing Dutch republic. Barbers had become physicians as well, with their own guild; the municipal government provided the guild with space and training facilities. So that they would not, in the words of the Greek physician

Galen, work the wood like blind men, they had to have in-struction in anatomy, for which the authorities were respon-sible. Many Dutch cities had spacious and cool premises available for the purpose, frequently in churches. Leiden, and later Amsterdam, had its own anatomical theater. (Amsterdam used its weigh-house, which also had room for the guildhall.) The instructor was a praelector, or lecturer, who described the procedure as he performed it, and was in fact a precursor of the medical professor. The city council appointed him, and members of the council who were also physicians often took the post themselves. Nicolaas Tulp was the third mayor of Amsterdam who was also a teacher of anatomy. The cadaver was invariably that of a criminal who had been executed—execution being the punishment then for many minor crimes.

Amsterdam had just opened its own athaeneum on Jan-uary 9, 1632 (a date still celebrated as the anniversary of its university), to rival the one in orthodox Leiden. A few weeks later Dr. Tulp's lesson would show that Amsterdam was second to none in anatomy. The lesson was a public occasion, attended by city councilors, surgeons, physicians, and other interested persons. For obvious reasons, since it sometimes lasted several days, it was given in the winter. Ironically, the cadaver was that of a man from Leiden who had been hanged in Amsterdam for repeated thefts of clothing.

In the painting, this deathly pale man, Aris Kindt, occupies the center of the canvas, but the viewer's attention is drawn to Dr. Nicolaas Tulp. He wears the black physician's hat and is lecturing, holding in his hand a pair of forceps; with them he lifts the muscles and tendons of the lower left arm. Seven senior members of the surgeons' guild observe. A book on anatomy appears in the lower right hand corner. But what is depicted is not what actually took place. Anatomy lessons always began with the dissection of the internal organs, because those were the first to deteriorate—never with the arm. Rembrandt has left the body intact to make the picture less gruesome and to focus attention on Dr. Tulp. Also, there is probably a symbolic relationship between the book on anatomy and Tulp's dissection.

The Belgian Andreas Vesalius had laid the foundations of modern anatomy with his research of a century before, and medical history is said to begin with his atlas, *De humanis corporis fabrica* (on the structure of the human body). Vesalius's text and woodcuts opened up a new world. For thirteen centuries the writings of Galen had been followed blindly, including the dictum that the body of a deceased person could not be violated for scientific purposes. As the physician to gladiators in Pergamum, Galen must have been in a position to observe many anatomical details, internal and external. But he derived his knowledge from pigs and apes, and his interpretations of what he found were based on untested theories. His authority, and then that of the medieval church, placed anatomy on the wrong track and kept it there until the time of Vesalius.

In all the editions of his work, Vesalius appears in a woodcut that shows him holding the dissected hand and arm of a cadaver. The hand was the first part of the body that Vesalius studied; the hand was also the surgeon's first instrument. And so Dr. Tulp is painted as Amsterdam's Vesalius, and it may be the latter's book that appears in the lower right-hand corner. In any event, Dr. Tulp's teacher in Leiden had studied with Vesalius in Padua and admired him. Dr. Tulp, in his public lesson, carries on that tradition.

The surgeons' guild had commissioned the painting for its meeting hall, an ancestral gallery of eminent anatomists painted by well-known artists. This was Rembrandt's first and most prestigious public commission since his recent move to Amsterdam, and, like the later *Nightwatch*, it has come to be regarded as an unconventional group portrait. The unconventionality applies not only to the pyramid of onlookers but also to the illumination of the cadaver. The focal point is the hand of the anatomist pointing to the specimen. Anatomists find the rendering of the underarm unconvincing because of the way the muscles and tendons are depicted; they seem to be painted from a source other than the actual autopsy, perhaps a woodcut or a specimen in the painter's studio.

The *Anatomy Lesson* also symbolizes mortality. It has a double meaning, as do so many paintings of the golden age. The commonplace points to a higher truth; the punishment for having sinned reminds mortal man of God. The Dutch dramatist Joost van den Vondel was referring poetically to anatomy when he said that God's wisdom courses through our sinews and arteries. The physician Jan Swammerdam, a few years later, saw the finger of God in the anatomy of a louse; and religious poetry permeates his book on the mayfly. Many Dutch operating theaters were adorned with skeletons bearing such mottoes as *homo bulla* (man is a bubble) as a warning to the living. But the *Anatomy Lesson* does more than provide an example of mortality. The dead man was not a person chosen at random but someone who had forfeited his life by committing a crime; and someone who was being allowed to atone for his sin by serving the good cause of medical instruction. Thus did the municipal government supply cadaver, anatomist, and moral precept all in one.

This is confirmed by the fact that Tulp was both mayor and anatomist. Like Rembrandt, he was a well-known figure in Amsterdam's canal district. He wrote about a number of new discoveries, sang the praises of the newly introduced tea

leaf as a universal remedy, and compiled the first pharmacopoeia, a guide to druggists in preparing medicines. Tulp had
a busy practice, which he attended to by means of his horse-
drawn coach and in his consulting room on the lower floor of
a house on the Keizersgracht. He spent half a century on the
Amsterdam city council, and in addition to all these activities
he was an astute physician whose professional accounts of
unusual and sometimes bizarre cases, written in Latin, gave
him a great reputation. He was no Leeuwenhoek and did not
advance his profession, but was still a shrewd and useful observer who opened the eyes of many contemporaries. He would
be forgotten if Rembrandt had not immortalized him as the
Vesalius of Amsterdam.

Life did not turn out that well for the original Vesalius.
The publication of his masterpiece on human anatomy, at the
age of twenty-eight, made him the founder of a new science,
but not without a struggle. His critics, faithful to the old
authority of Galen, did not believe the evidence of their eyes,
and Vesalius had to endure harsh condemnation of his work
and methods. Embittered, he gave up scientific research,
burned his notes, and became the personal physician to the
Spanish monarchs Charles V and Philip II. At the court he
once treated a nobleman with a mysterious ailment; when the
patient died, he asked for permission to perform an autopsy.
It was rumored that Vesalius opened the chest cavity and found
the heart still beating. On the strength of this, the Spanish
Inquisition charged him with sinning against God and man,
and would have had him hanged if the king had not intervened.
As penance, Vesalius was compelled to make a pilgrimage to
Jerusalem. On the return voyage he was shipwrecked, and died
in 1564 on Zákinthos, an island off the coast of the Pelopon-
nesus. The story of the beating heart may be apocryphal, but

it is an intriguing one—at the boundary between life and death, the founder of the science of anatomy makes a mistake.

AS MEDICAL SCIENCE PROGRESSED, the public anatomy lesson was discontinued. In the seventeenth century, physicians, well read but without practical experience, observed their patients and tried to alleviate their suffering. By the eighteenth century, the emphasis switched to practical experience; the control of epidemics, public health, and the diagnosis of the disease while the patient was still alive. Nevertheless, anatomical knowledge remained the basis for such common procedures as setting bones, bleeding, splinting, and bandaging. That is why the British surgeons' guilds were given the monopoly on autopsies of hanged criminals—although the autopsies were of scant practical benefit for things like amputations or kidney stones.

Operations were performed by filthy surgeons on fully conscious patients lying on wooden tables and bandaged with dirty linen. The principles of infection of wounds were unknown, often with fatal results. The medical student Charles Darwin, after witnessing two operations in Edinburgh, changed his mind about becoming a doctor. In the early 1800s, hospitals were places for the indigent sick to die, inns of death for the wounded, the unwell, and women in childbirth. Although there was some medical experimentation with live patients, hospital managements and the authorities permitted this on the deceased only in exceptional cases. Usually, relatives collected the remains intact, after paying up, or the deceased was given a pauper's burial. Surgeons had their anatomical opportunity only while the patients were alive. The exception was executed criminals, who as an additional disgrace were obliged to leave their dead bodies to science, which did not even have to bury them.

In the eighteenth century, physicians and professors began to ask the municipal authorities for permission to perform at least four autopsies annually on persons who died in a hospital. The hospital regents consistently opposed this. The state argued that the indigent had profited from their hospital stay and could settle their account, after their death, with an anatomy lesson, but the hospital administrators preferred payment in cash. They did not attach much importance to instruction and education anyway, and the training of surgeons, much of it designed to meet the needs of ships at sea, seemed to interest them hardly at all. Their main concern was that the indigent should have only the most primitive facilities; anything more might cost too much. In addition, the Christian conviction that the dead body should be kept intact until the day of Resurrection played a part in all this. The earthly tent had been folded but should not be cut to ribbons, unless it housed a criminal, who had forfeited his ticket of admission to eternity.

Not until after 1800, when improved medical education, research, and nursing led to the development of the modern clinic, did anatomy take its rightful place in the science of pathology. Speculations about the structure and functioning of the human body gave way to actual observations and descriptions of disorders at the bedside, and to the search for their physical causes on the operating table. One of the founders of the Vienna medical school, pathologist-anatomist Karl von Rokitansky, performed more than 60,000 autopsies in the course of his career. His students, who included Ignaz Semmelweis, commuted between dissecting table and bedside; the dead made it possible to understand the living. Often the future doctors also transmitted the fatal puerperal fever, the particular terror of indigent mothers who had to give birth in hospitals. Semmelweis discerned this peril of the anatomy lesson and demonstrated how to avoid it by the simple expedient of washing the hands. But hardly anyone believed him, and he died insane, on the fringes of the medical profession.

British anatomists of the eighteenth century, like those elsewhere, had to be satisfied with the cadavers of the hanged, but even for this they needed the permission of the authorities. Though hangings were numerous, the many anatomy schools and the surgeons' guilds had an inadequate supply of bodies; the condemned, the executioners, and their assistants all had to be bribed in order to obtain cadavers. The public, with mixed feelings of sensitivity and distaste, did not care for the imposition of the added punishment of dissection. Also, the drama of death by hanging nurtured superstitions, that the blood of one executed, for example, could heal epilepsy and leprosy, or that touching the corpse could cure glandular tuberculosis, ulcers, and tumors. The crush of interested parties around the gallows must have been considerable.

A simpler method of acquiring study material for the anatomists was body snatching. Paupers were usually buried in communal graves, and their corpses could easily be taken from their coffins. And the surgeons' guilds paid well. London had entire gangs of so-called resurrectionists; at fixed rates, they stole bodies from mortuaries. The famous physicians John and William Hunter were involved in such activities. John Hunter bribed an undertaker to obtain the corpse of an Irish giant who had made his name as a circus attraction in London. Many anatomists were after the body, if only to add it to their collections of curiosities, but it ended up in Hunter's hands, in spite of the man's wish to be buried at sea. The unfortunate Irishman's skeleton is still on display at the entrance to the Royal College of Surgeons in London, as a preview of the complete Hunter collection housed there.

The body snatcher did his work silently at night, tidied

the grave, delivered to regular customers, and kept his mouth shut. If he was caught, the penalty was a minor one, because a corpse was nobody's property and its theft, purchase, or sale had no juridical significance. And since the graves were those of the poor, there was little recourse for individuals. The well-to-do had themselves buried in a sort of posthumous safe—cast-iron coffins with padlocks or wooden coffins lowered into metal cages. Historian Ruth Richardson, who has written a chilling and informative book about body snatching, is of the opinion that for decades no pauper's grave in any English university town was safe from grave robbers. She adds that the market value of the corpses was established in sinister bargaining between the thieves and the surgeons.

Public disgust increased as the number of thefts rose. In Aberdeen, a new anatomical institute was set on fire after the discovery that its staff was treating corpses like garbage. When it came out that important hospitals were giving their indigent patients mock burials and then retrieving bodies at night for use in the dissecting room, the House of Commons finally appointed a commission of inquiry. Physicians of high repute protested that medical science could not advance without anatomical knowledge, since the body's functions were based on its structure. Anatomical study, they said, benefited the living, and this worthy end justified less than fastidious means. If there were objections to that point of view, let the law provide a more acceptable way of meeting the demand for corpses. The initiator of this position was Jeremy Bentham, the philosopher of social benefit, who believed that by reforms of the law society could bring the greatest possible good to the greatest number of people. A typical man of the Enlightenment, he had no doubts about the scientific necessity of anatomy, and by the early age of twenty-one had already bequeathed his body to science. Bentham argued that the needy in hospitals, because they could not pay for their care, had tacitly consented to autopsy in the event of death. In due course they would be given a Christian burial, he added—a considerable improvement over the current practice of doing it the other way around.

As the Parliamentary commission went to work in 1828, an incident in Edinburgh greatly inflamed the debate. An Irishwoman without money or food, who had come to Edinburgh in search of a lost son and was begging in a bar, was taken home by one of the customers, a man named Burke. At a party there she was given food and drink, and later that night Burke murdered her. The crime was discovered the next day, and Burke confessed. It turned out that Burke and an accomplice named Hare had done away with sixteen unfortunate wanderers after luring them from the streets and getting them drunk. The bodies had been delivered, at a high price per body, to the eminent surgeon and anatomist Robert Knox. On the strength of Hare's confession, Burke was hanged in public, in the presence of a cheering Scottish throng. As a further punishment, his corpse was consigned to the dissectors, and the judge stipulated that his skeleton be preserved as a reminder of the crime. So the dealer in cadavers himself became an anatomy lesson, which was attended the first day by two thousand students and the next day by thirty thousand curious citizens of Edinburgh.

Dr. Knox admitted no guilt, although he must have suspected that all those fresh bodies, not laid out and sometimes showing signs of a violent end, had not come by the customary route, from a hospital, a cheap inn, or needy relatives. The commission was unable—or unwilling—to prove his complicity, and he went free.

Burke's public execution and dissection demonstrated con-
clusively that an anatomy lesson could be made an additional
punishment for a capital crime. But that did not make any
easier the adoption of new legislation on autopsies, legislation
designed to expand the concept of dissecting criminals to
include the indigent. While criminals could be said to have
lost any entitlement to respect in death, the indigent were
being asked to forfeit that right in exchange for the free care
they received during their final illness. Parliament rejected a
first version of the proposed legislation on the ground that the
indigent were not criminals and were entitled to a Christian
burial. Also, it seemed to be the wrong time to adopt such a
law; there was great public anxiety over crime, and the poor
had already been deprived of many rights. Some physicians
insisted on the voluntary agreement of indigent patients to
dissection in the event of death, and a few of them set the
example themselves. But virtually every self-respecting Englishman considered it wrong for a pauper to be treated after death
like a villain. Finally, in 1832, after lengthy debate, Parliament
adopted a law permitting hospital and poorhouse administrators, subject to certain legal controls, to make the corpses of
indigent patients available to the dissecting room without the
obligation of burial. The institutions thus saved on funeral
expenses, and the dissectors got their corpses. The anatomy
lesson now ceased to be a posthumous punishment and became
instead a worthwhile—albeit compulsory—way for the dis-
possessed to express their thanks for services rendered.

While the last legislative touches were being put to the
anatomy law, its spiritual father, Bentham, died. He was a
famous man with many followers, and it was public knowledge
that he had willed his body to science. Friends and relatives
were invited to an anatomy lesson in London, to be conducted

by Bentham's friend, the anatomist Southwood Smith, as the deceased had requested. Under the terms of Bentham's will, his body was to be delivered to Smith, who would dissect it, mount and clothe the skeleton, and dry out the head. Bentham had owned for twenty years the glass eyes that were to stare out from his dessicated skull. He considered his remains useful for dissection; his skeleton, on the other hand, if properly preserved, could be his monument—or, as he put it himself, his auto-icon.

The funeral oration by Southwood Smith, delivered during a tumultuous thunderstorm, must have been masterly, because he was also a lay preacher. The sermon drew the affluent audience's attention to the worthy and rational example set by his departed friend. Later, Smith prepared the skeleton with great care, secured the joints with copper wire, and dried the head in an oven. The result was not particularly appealing, due to a lack of expression; a French doctor made a more flattering wax model. According to Ruth Richardson's book, the actual head rests in a vault of University College in London. Southwood Smith donated his reconstructed friend to that institution, and it stashed him away in a back room.

Bentham had thought of the auto-icon as a lasting monument; had envisioned temples set in avenues of trees and filled with auto-icons of good people and bad—a sort of anatomical homily. He had many ideas about ways of preserving them, and even saw them as characters in historical tableaux. A rationalist, Bentham could conceive of how the dead might be of benefit to the living, and not only as solemn reminders of mortality. He wanted to be his own relic, visited by admirers, an example for others to follow. In addition, by bequeathing himself to an able and trustworthy anatomist, he escaped the collecting mania of surgeons and body snatchers. His example, however, was not followed; the new law provided for enough corpses from the poor, making it unnecessary for the rich to bestir themselves. And time took its toll of his auto-icon.

Jeremy Bentham is regarded today as an eminent pragmatic philosopher, not an eighteenth-century eccentric—although the latter is something an Englishman would not object to. But Bentham's real rehabilitation occurred in 1981, when, with the help of textile experts, the skeleton was beautifully restored, the clothing dry-cleaned, the moth holes repaired, the coat and suspenders reconditioned. Wearing clean white gaiters, hat on head and walking stick in hand, he sits once more in a mahogany display cabinet at University College. The glass door is opened for a brief daily airing, to freshen him, and he is ready to receive visitors at all times. Those visitors may be surprised by such posthumous egocentricity, but let us hope they also admire him for having, of his own free will and in the face of every prejudice, promoted the anatomy lesson as a benefit to humanity, not a punishment.

THE PATHOLOGIST-ANATOMISTS OF TODAY speak of the autopsy as the final consultation. It is performed mainly for purposes of instruction, to confirm a clinical diagnosis that may have been incomplete or inaccurate. For many reasons, it is not the importance but the methodology of the autopsy that has changed drastically.

Better diagnostic techniques, such as X rays, tissue analysis, and a multitude of laboratory tests, leave few questions unanswered, and the deceased, usually elderly and succumbing after a long illness and a multiplicity of afflictions, generally does not provide any surprises. What is more often cause for astonishment is that such an emaciated and ravaged body contained life only a short while before. Pathological anatomists themselves usually show little interest in autopsies, a relatively primitive method of observation today, preferring more subtle microscopic methods.

Dutch law says that people own their bodies and that without their permission, government authorities and others have virtually no right of disposal over them. The body of the deceased belongs to his heirs, to dispose of within the limitations imposed by the law and the wishes of the deceased. Thus the permission of relatives is required before an autopsy can be performed, and they frequently refuse. A doctor's interest in the patient, which can begin before the patient's birth, is difficult for them to accept when it extends beyond the deathbed. Enough, they feel, is enough. The number of autopsies performed in teaching hospitals has dropped below 30 percent of total deaths, and there is much concern about monitoring the medical procedures considered necessary for postmortem examinations. Courts can order dissection only in the event of unnatural death: a suspicion of medical error, an accident, or an indictable offense. Not for the edification of the physician, in other words, but to detect a crime. Autopsy is again linked to crime.

The current attitude toward autopsy derives from our way of looking at death. It used to be, one died; now, one "passes away." The former seemed a more active process. The seriously ill were aware of their impending death, prepared themselves for it, gathered their friends and relatives around them for a last farewell. If at all possible, one made one's peace with God and man, closed one's eyes, expelled the last breath, and died—stiffened—in one's own bed, in one's own house. One was laid out before being carried to the grave, there to await some form of eternal life as recompense for a too brief and often unhappy existence. Dying was also a lesson on how to live, a model of leave-taking and hope. In the cemeteries of many religious houses the headstones omit the date of birth and are engraved only with the date of death, for that is when the new life begins.

Since Jeremy Bentham's day, if not before, such beliefs have largely disappeared. Dying no longer offers moral instruction; at best, it can serve a useful purpose in supplying organs or parts of them, ranging from the cornea to the heart, from the kidneys to the liver, for transplanting, giving some of those condemned to die a new lease on life.

Meanwhile, like Vesalius in his apocryphal last autopsy, we are having difficulty determining, in the process of dying, the exact moment of death. The classic characteristics of death, the cessation of the heart and of breathing, have become reversible; those functions can be assumed, partially and temporarily, by machines. We now link death to the brain, which is vulnerable to lack of blood and oxygen. Brain death has been further narrowed to the cessation of the functioning of the brain stem, that service hatch for the transmission of all stimuli from and to the cerebrum.

In Anglo-Saxon countries, the practice is for doctors to determine brain-stem death by such simple bedside means as checking the patient's breathing, reflexes, and the pupils of the eye. The French, less sure of themselves, require repeated electroencephalograms indicating the complete cessation of activity in the cerebral cortex. The Germans prescribe, even on the deathbed, an X ray with a counterstain, to indicate that the brain is no longer being supplied with blood. It is something of an academic debate between those who rely on common sense and those who prefer to be more precise. The position of the Dutch may offer a compromise that, without requiring a diagnosis of brain death, will satisfy both sides: it is normally sufficient to wait a day for all the regulatory systems to cease functioning, and that is true death.

If the patient is young and has been healthy, however, his death has special significance for the new science of healing by transplants. The moment brain death occurs—no matter how it is established—medical interest becomes intense. Here is a potential organ donor, and potential recipients are waiting. Our medical skill does not point to a cadaver, as Dr. Tulp did, but to the unseen dead brain stem.

No one can make the decision for us, to donate our organs. Yet, as with the poor of London, there is an unspoken assumption that those who are about to die should show their gratitude for the care they received by making a gift of their usable parts, which otherwise would go to waste. There is no shortage of potential donors; it is necessary only to wait for a traffic accident or a stroke. But only the initiated can detect the death of the brain stem; it is not evident to those at the bedside, who see the patient still connected to the monitor and respirator as before. Often they say goodbye to someone who appears to be alive, but in whom death has already taken place, invisibly. The anatomy lesson brain death teaches is that any further medical attention to the patient is pointless, but that a new hope for life has become available for another. And so the transplant teams remain on the alert.

What is left after transplantation are mortal remains, which served their purpose for the patient and possibly for others. Increasingly today, the remains are cremated rather than buried. In Holland, the preference for cremation is close to a century old, although at one time it aroused as much indignation as body snatching did. At the first Dutch cremation, in 1914, the relatives of the deceased were taken to court. In the near future, cremation will be an environmental necessity.

There have been changes in the way we regard death and the discarded body, and changes also in the anatomy lesson. It is constantly teaching us something new, but it is also teaching us what it always has—that death can hold a mirror up to life.

Eternal Youth

THE STOCKY, BEARDED PROFESSOR addressing a learned Parisian audience on June 1, 1889, was as famous as his colleagues Louis Pasteur and Jean-Martin Charcot. He was the successor to Claude Bernard, the patron saint of medical researchers, and he occupied the chair of experimental medicine at the Collège de France. At Harvard and in New York, he had done research on the central nervous system. Along with the work of Charcot and others, his experiments had made French neurology internationally renowned. Paris was the mecca of neuropsychiatry then. In 1885 Freud had worked there for six months, living on a meager travel grant, in order to take in all the latest developments.

The speaker's lecture was devoted entirely to himself. His name was Charles Brown-Séquard, and each new generation of medical students is still being taught the syndrome (semi-lateral damage to the spinal cord) named after him. On that summer afternoon in Paris, however, he was talking about something else. At the age of seventy-two, crowned with laurels from French and foreign academies, Brown-Séquard felt old and tired; he could work in his laboratory only a few hours at a time and had difficulty climbing stairs. In late May, after a variety of experiments on animals, he had given himself eight injections. They had had a virtually instantaneous rejuvenating effect, restoring powers that he had gradually lost over the preceding ten years. That was the subject of his lecture.

Brown-Séquard was not one to imagine things; he was a painstaking researcher, even when he was his own subject. He had measured his increased muscular strength with a dynamometer (a metal spring compressed by the hand); had noted the jet of his urine before and after the injections, being careful to consume equal amounts of food and drink; had kept a record of his bowel movements. His mental powers had increased. He could work for hours in his laboratory. He could run up and down stairs. The eight injections of testicular extracts had made him feel sixty again, he said. He had used the testicles of dogs or guinea pigs, along with their blood, sperm, and spermatic cord, which he pulverized in a solution of glycerin. The mixture, after standing for half a day, was diluted with distilled water and filtered. The filtrate, in an amount equal to one-quarter of a testicle, was injected under the skin.

He undertook the experiment, he said, in the belief that it would improve the function of the central nervous system and the spinal cord. That appeared to have happened, as evidenced by the increased mobility of the bladder and bowels. The testicle played an important role in personal vitality, he maintained, citing the deleterious effect on eunuchs and elderly men of absent or scarcely functional testicles, as well as the consequences of heavy sperm loss due to excessive masturbation or sexual intercourse. Elderly men could be revitalized by injections of male sperm. But Brown-Séquard, for all his frankness, was a true Victorian; he divulged nothing about the effect of his injections on his own sex life.

The report of his self-experiment was straightforward and called on his colleagues, in accordance with established practice, to see whether they could reproduce the results. He did not rule out autosuggestion. To test on a human being what he had learned in his laboratory, using rabbits and guinea pigs, he had willingly made himself the first subject. It had proved difficult to assess the effects of the testicular extracts on the animals, so it became obvious that he would have to try them on himself.

Medical self-experimentation has a long tradition and has on occasion met with great success. In 1929 a young German medical assistant, Werner Forssmann, put a catheter into a vein in his arm and pushed it all the way to the right atrium of his heart, and took an X ray to prove it. In 1956 Forssmann—by this time an obscure country doctor—was awarded a Nobel Prize for having been the first to perform a catheterization of the heart. Stubborn conviction, curiosity, lack of a suitable test animal, and a knack for experimentation have led many researchers to try remedies on themselves, to go on strange diets, to infect or vaccinate themselves—in order to show the world the effectiveness, safety, or significance of something. One such case:

Sigmund Freud, shortly before his stay in Paris, became acquainted in the laboratory with cocaine, which had only recently been isolated from the leaves of the coca plant. A medicine in search of an ailment, cocaine was being tried as a cure for morphine addiction, alcoholism, and severe exhaustion. It was administered to Bavarian soldiers on maneuvers, without their knowledge, to counteract fatigue. An Italian neurologist, trying it on himself, had recorded an improvement in such vital functions as breathing and circulation. Freud began to use it on himself, measuring the effects with a dynamometer, as Brown-Séquard did, keeping track of his reaction times, noting numbness in his tongue and lips. During this troubled and poverty-stricken period of his apprenticeship he found that the cocaine improved his mood and controlled his stomach cramps. Freud told a friend who was an ophthalmic surgeon about the numbing effect on the mucous membranes, and the surgeon, experimenting, found that cocaine was an excellent local anesthetic for eye operations. Freud wrote up his self-experiments and recommended the use of cocaine for a variety of afflictions. This proved to be a valuable contribution to the pharmacology of the nervous system—but at the cost of a personal addiction that lasted for years. Soon after his experiments, Freud met the neurological surgeon Charcot in Paris and was deeply impressed by his precise observations and the fact that he gave greater weight to clinical experience than to theory. Freud would remember Charcot with great respect all his life, would even name his eldest son after him. Invited to a reception in the great man's home, Freud, a young apprentice in a bad suit and with bad French, dared to go only after a dose of cocaine. Injections of vegetable matter, not only animal, could provide vitality.

On the strength of Brown-Séquard's reputation, his message spread through the medical world, which busily began to repeat the experiment on the ill, the infirm, and the elderly. In some cases the area of the injection became infected, and in many others there were no discernible results, but interest in organ extracts grew. For doctors were learning that organs did not only excrete lymph, gastric acid, and urine, they also secreted valuable substances into the bloodstream. Biological life depends on the coordination of the nervous system, but in addition on certain chemicals, which in 1902 British physiologist Ernest Henry Starling would call hormones.

In 1885, Joseph von Mering and Oskar Minkowski, in Strasbourg, removed the entire pancreas from a dog in order to study the organ. The dog lived, and when a student noticed the large number of flies settling on its urine, Minkowski discovered that the urine contained an unusual amount of sugar.

The dog proved to have diabetes; with its pancreas removed, the blood-sugar-regulating hormone we know as insulin had also disappeared. A few years later, it was found that an extract from the thyroid of a sheep could be used in a preparation that helped those suffering from a thyroid malfunction. The interest in glandular therapy, which Brown-Séquard had initiated, was in fact the beginning of modern endocrinology. It would be years before practical applications became available, ranging from insulin to the growth hormones, from thyroid-gland extracts to cortisone, but the experimental foundation had been laid. For Brown-Séquard's elixir of life, however, one did not have to wait. It was being concocted in laboratories of all descriptions, with great hopes of success and commercial gain.

Glandular therapy disappeared from the medical arsenal within a few decades, because the primitive extracts proved to have no noticeable effect. Their active ingredients remained unknown, as did the manner in which they were absorbed by the body. Biochemical regulation of the body had to wait for purer drugs. Brown-Séquard's testicular extract was ahead of its time; it would not be until the 1930s that the Amsterdam pharmacologist Laqueur isolated the active ingredient—testosterone. On the other hand, the fact that testicles had something to do with vitality, virility, and sexual potency had been known since the eunuchs of antiquity. Animal testicles in wine or honey were traditionally served for their stimulating effect, and many an old pharmacopoeia contains some word on this subject.

BY THE END of the nineteenth century, experimentation with animals to study the mechanism of diseases and test remedies and vaccines made controlled scientific research possible and anecdote and alchemy obsolete. Life expectancy was increasing as a result of better nutrition, hygiene, and housing; more people lived to middle age and beyond. During *la belle époque*, with prosperity and leisure time went the desire to remain vigorous throughout one's life and keep at bay the decrepitude of old age. And since vitality derived from the testicles, rejuvenation cures focused on male virility. Women of course occupied a subordinate position in that society— but, also, the male was more convenient an object of study than the female, whose ovaries could not be reached or manipulated, at least not for another century, without risk.

The first to resume the experiments of Brown-Séquard was a young Viennese physiologist, Eugen Steinach, director of the biological laboratory of the Academy of Sciences. His hypothesis was that the physical and mental maturation of youths derived from the pubertal gland: the testes. Perhaps the reactivation of testicular function in old age could result in a second youth.

Steinach began experimenting in 1912 with old rats, mangy, skinny, apathetic, and oblivious to females in heat. He restored their limp and empty testicles by ligation of the spermatic cord and lateral veins on both sides of the groin. The result: hypertrophy of the cells in the tissues that produced testosterone, while the production of sperm cells ceased. Male sexual characteristics persisted, but the rats were sterile. Steinach believed that the ligation of the spermatic duct would increase the flow of blood to the testicles, with a corresponding increase in hormone production. He was right. The rats' fur became thicker; they gained weight; they grew more sprightly and aggressive; and their sexual appetite returned, even when the ligation was on only one side. Steinach called the procedure an autoplastic defense against old age—the use of the body's own biological resources. In cases where this treatment failed, he transplanted the testicles of young rats into the abdomen or abdominal wall of the old ones, again with a measure of success. The rats lived a year beyond their normal life span of three.

Steinach turned to human subjects. With the assistance of a Viennese surgeon named Lichtenstern, on November 1, 1918, he operated on an emaciated, listless Viennese laborer—the first man to undergo the double ligation of his spermatic ducts. For two months there was no change in the man's condition. Then he seemed to pick up, had a better appetite, developed strength in his muscles, and went back to work. His skin and hair glistened. As if reborn, this first crown witness of the rejuvenation process strutted around Vienna. The Steinach operation, a simple intervention that held out the lure of an elixir of life, became fashionable on the fringes of conventional medical practice. Old gentlemen who could afford it quietly visited certain surgeons. Some of the surgeons eventually publicized their results—even though it was months after the operation before they could claim to find any beneficial effect, and then in only a third of the cases. Many people considered Steinach a charlatan, and he himself was well aware how limited his experiments were, for research on hormones and aging was too complex for one man short of funds. He hoped that others, working in well-financed research institutes, would continue his work.

That happened with the arrival on the scene of Dr. Serge Voronoff, an eccentric Russian who had studied in Paris and after a period of roving through Africa had followed Claude Bernard and Brown-Séquard as head of the experimental laboratory of the Collège de France. Voronoff became proficient in surgically transplanting skin, thyroid glands, bone, and ovaries in laboratory animals. He would amaze the world with his testicular transplants in human beings.

Unicellular organisms could reproduce indefinitely as the Pasteur Institute in Paris had discovered, but complex human tissues stiffened as they aged and required some kind of treatment if they were to remain vital and youthful. As a surgeon in North Africa, Voronoff had become interested in the condition of castrated boys, whom he found to be mentally and physically retarded. The cure for tuberculosis of the genitals was castration, and after a few years the castrated males exhibited poor memory and loss of concentration. Also, Voronoff had never heard of a eunuch living beyond sixty. His conclusion: the loss of the internal secretions of the testes hastened old age and shortened one's life. The testicles of the old, therefore, were in need of regeneration. But the Steinach operation was too uncertain in its results; and the transplanting of young testicles under the abdominal wall didn't help much, either, because without a good blood supply the tissue rapidly deteriorated, as Voronoff's experiments proved. And vascular surgery was not advanced enough for tiny connections to be made.

Voronoff devised a new technique. He took testicle tissue, cut it into thin slices, and placed the slices inside the membranous lining of the patient's testicle. He scored this lining with a surgical knife or nail, to stimulate the formation of new ducts to feed the four small sections of the transplant. But the most sensational aspect of Voronoff's procedure was the testicle donor. In Vienna, a few surgeons had used the testicles of young men that had not descended properly during puberty. Voronoff was using monkey testicles.

He was well prepared for his experiments, having performed hundreds of operations on goats and bulls, and his 1926 book on rejuvenation contains beautiful photographs of men and animals before and after treatment. His post at the respected French laboratory ensured assistance from all quarters. In addition, between 1913 and 1915, in treating two boys who suffered since birth from sluggish thyroid glands and the accompanying mental and physical retardation, he had transplanted the thyroid of a chimpanzee, the animal most closely related to humans. Chimpanzees were hard to obtain, however, so in later operations he used a lobe of the thyroid gland taken from the patient's mother—though he much preferred using chimpanzees.

In June of 1920, Voronoff performed his first animal-human testicle transplant. Over the next five years he and his pupils performed three hundred of them throughout the world. True, only microscopic examination could determine whether the transplant had taken, and what man was willing to sacrifice his regained youth on the altar of science? One plucky tailor who had received a transplant in 1922 did allow two of the four transplanted sections of tissue to be removed, and the tissue proved to be healthy.

The donor problem appeared insuperable, until it was discovered that small apes such as the macaque monkey were also suitable. Macaques lived in troops in North Africa and were easy to catch. Nevertheless, by 1926 Voronoff was urging that this resource be used sparingly—and that if necessary the monkeys be bred, like ostriches. Three years earlier, he had performed forty-three transplants, half of them in patients under sixty. These included medical colleagues, academics, architects, authors, and industrialists, many of whom claimed to feel reborn and allowed before-and-after pictures to be taken. For years they would write testimonials about their health, appearance, and sexual appetites.

Brown-Séquard had been a methodical researcher, and Steinach had done no more than extrapolate from rats to humans. But Voronoff was a flamboyant missionary—a miracle worker for randy old men. The fact that traditional medicine did not take him seriously only added to his renown. In commercial pharmaceutical laboratories and in universities, the quest for the unadulterated hormone of youth continued, because no one was comfortable with surgery and the introduction of tissue from another species.

In the 1920s, insulin and the hormone of the anterior pituitary gland were isolated. The most important male and female sex hormones were discovered in the '30s, as was the fact that men produce some female and women some male hormones. Testosterone and its compounds could have been refined further, but they proved to have almost no application, only in rare cases where, because of illness or a defect, the patient's own production was insufficient. As a medicine, the male hormone had undesirable side effects. In the '50s, derivatives of it were discovered to be better stimulants of protein building and not as masculinizing. Prescribed for short periods—after exhaustion, a serious operation, or decalcification of the bones—they were moderately beneficial. These, the anabolic steroids, today are taken primarily by athletes, because they promote rapid increase in muscle size. They also involve the risk of kidney damage, rupture of the tendons, and sterility. The elixir of life, in the process of biochemical refinement, had evaporated.

THE DESIRE FOR YOUTH persists even when the end is in sight. In 1934, William Butler Yeats was sixty-nine and alone. The Irish poet had won the Nobel Prize but lost the patroness who for forty years had supported him in his writing and his political battles. He suffered from high blood pressure and a failing heart, and his creativity seemed to be drying up. Yeats, a mystic, with a distaste for impersonal science, had heard talk about the rejuvenation procedure. To the consternation of his friends, he found an Australian sexologist in London's Harley Street, who performed the Steinach operation on him in the spring of 1934. The operation worked. In his letters, Yeats said that he had regained sexual desire and fallen in love with a young poetess. Dubliners began calling him the "gland old man." He wrote new poems. One of these, "The Spur," reads:

> You think it horrible that lust and rage
> Should dance attention upon my old age.
> They were not such a plague when I was young;
> What else have I to spur me into song?

He compiled the *Oxford Book of Modern Verse* and worked on his collected poems as if he had a new lease on life. Yeats died five years later, of heart failure, on the Riviera.

As the science of endocrinology advanced, reliance on human or animal testicles, in the search for the elixir of life, waned. Eternal youth has become the goal of women, too. The female hormone estrogen, synthetically produced, replaces what the body can no longer supply after menopause, and it seems to be a panacea for wrinkles, bone loss, irritation, and depression. But organotherapy, employing tissues and cells, though now on the periphery of medical science, remains the stock-in-trade of fashionable quacks. The Swiss surgeon Niehans, fascinated by the idea of gland transplants, in 1931 began to inject patients with a solution of cells obtained from young farm animals. Fetal cells in particular were supposed to have the capacity for rejuvenating diseased or aging organs. By freeze-drying the fetal cells of sheep, suspensions were made that could be absorbed under the skin or in muscles. Blood cells would then break down the sheep cells and carry the resulting macromolecules to the appropriate organs, which they would regenerate.

After the war, cell therapy was pursued mainly in German-speaking countries and used for a variety of ailments, especially premature aging. Niehans, the foremost proponent, was such a dignified figure that one hesitates to apply the word charlatan. Indeed, his Swiss clinic was patronized by such eminent persons as German chancellor Konrad Adenauer, Pope Pius XII, and the Duke and Duchess of Windsor. Another asylum against aging could be found in Romania, where Dr. Ana Aslan restored youth to the elderly by injecting them with procaine, a local anesthetic. The gerontocracy of eastern Europe went there to stay alive and healthy. Dr. Niehans's work was carried on some years later in Rome by the former transplant surgeon Dr. Christiaan Barnard. No longer physically able to perform surgery, he became a magnet for those seeking eternal youth in the Eternal City.

No one wishes to age; everyone wishes to stay young. The question is at what price. For eternal youth is an illusion that requires other illusions. Of the search for the elixir of life that Brown-Séquard embarked on so conscientiously, little remains. The one by-product of it still with us is the ligation of the spermatic duct, the vasectomy. And that constitutes the ultimate surgical intervention, since it rules out the chance to rejuvenate ourselves—through our offspring.

"Viva il Coltello"

THE SENIOR MOZART did not care much for his employers, the archbishops of Salzburg. So he spent more than half his time traveling with his wonder child, Wolfgang Amadeus, the darling of royal courts and a good source of income. In 1770, on their second trip to Italy, the junior Mozart, thirteen years old, was paid ten times as much as his father. The nobleman with whom they stayed gave them an introduction to the Vatican, and the pope decorated Wolfgang Amadeus with the Order of the Golden Spur. The child's dexterity at the keyboard, as well as the improvisations and inventions he produced so effortlessly, amazed the most jaded Italian audiences. In Bologna, on the way home, he was admitted to the Accademia Filharmonica on the strength of a recommendation from a priest named Giovanni Battista Martini, and after passing a test in composition. Father Martini, himself a mediocre composer and choirmaster, paid the entrance fees out of his own pocket, because he recognized genius when he saw it—as Antonio Salieri would later, in Vienna. After hearing Mozart in Naples, another prelate wrote that he was, and would always be, a prodigy.

The visit to Bologna, a city of music lovers, was a success, but Mozart was not the only celebrity there. In a handsome classical villa lived an old prodigy, Father Martini's closest friend and the best-known person in Bologna. Young Mozart had to make the rounds of the royal courts, but elector and emperor

ents. There were even castrations of babies and toddlers, although the operation itself did not guarantee a good singing voice. The loss of the testicles was usually ascribed to some mishap, such as a fall or an animal bite.

The operation affected not just the voice. The hair on the head became fuller, the beard failed to grow, and the breasts developed significantly. Castrati were often tall, became obese in time, had wonderful mobility and boyish speaking voices. In some cases, when the breasts grew large, the figure became quite feminine. Sometimes castrati wore women's clothes and sang androgynous or female roles. A good singer could earn a great deal of money, could take care of his parents in their old age. If it turned out that a castrato could not sing, it was a catastrophe, a sacrifice to art made in vain. One alternative was to become a male prostitute, although homosexuality among the castrati appears to have been relatively rare. Like the eunuchs of old, they were considered safe company for women, whom they might make love to but could not make pregnant. With marriage forbidden them by law and the Church, the castrati were reduced to having affairs, often with women of consequence who out of boredom or curiosity were looking for adventure. Many of the castrati were regarded as pompous, vain, pretentious—but these were attributes which they had in common with opera singers in full possession of their endocrine functions. Some, on the other hand, like Farinelli, were praised for their generosity, good character, and refinement. Since the castrati were so different from others, left out of so many things, and had only one talent, their behavior was probably a form of self-defense.

Farinelli, whose real name was Carlo Broschi, was born in the Kingdom of Naples into a family of merchants that valued music highly. His eldest brother became a well-regarded composer. Carlo, as a small boy, was found to have a lovely voice, and a fall from a horse became the pretext for an operation. The singing angel secured a place with the famous voice teacher Porpora, who had been a pupil of Scarlatti. Like Mozart's father, Porpora recognized the child's genius and gave him the most rigorous and thorough musical training possible. Farinelli's debut in Rome was followed by a triumphal tour through Italy and, later, equally successful appearances in Vienna and the German principalities. These were the rungs on his ladder to success. Farinelli carried with him a valise filled with bravura arias, which he added as signature tunes to the score of the role he was performing. Italian opera then was really a concert in disguise, designed to let the leading singer shine. Such traveling led to reviews passed on by word of mouth, to a reputation, to a permanent position at court as a singer or a music teacher, and those who made good money and saved it could face old age with equanimity. The less successful sang in choirs or chapels as long as their voices held out. Of the thousands who underwent castration annually, few achieved any real prosperity.

The Italians adored their castrati, were the only ones at first to use them in bel canto roles, but soon this invention was exported to all the opera houses of Europe. *"Viva il coltello"* (long live the knife), the Italians would call out after a fine performance, and they were now not the only enthusiasts. When Farinelli arrived in London in 1734, not yet thirty years old, the city lay at his feet. Compared with the Italian provinces or the princely households of Germany, London was the center of the world, and it gave him a royal reception. The Prince of Wales presented him with a snuffbox and a sum of money, and the public was beside itself. Farinelli stayed almost three years.

He might have spent the rest of his life there if he had not accepted an invitation from Elizabeth Farnese, the Italian wife of the Spanish king, Philip V, to come to Madrid. Philip, whom Louis XIV had placed on the throne as the first Bourbon monarch, was a depressive who eventually refused to bathe, dress, or even get out of bed. He was subject to fits of anger, during which he would beat the queen, his father confessor, or his personal physician. Philip lived in constant fear of being poisoned, and he paid little attention to affairs of state. Queen Elizabeth had once, in her homeland, heard Farinelli sing, and she was hoping for a miracle. She invited him to the somber Spanish court to see if he could rouse the king from his melancholy, as David with his harp had diverted Saul.

Farinelli did sing, in a room next to the royal bedchamber, and the miracle took place. The king was enchanted, asked who the singer was, wanted to reward him. As the queen had instructed him to do, Farinelli requested that the king get out of bed, shave himself, bathe, and dress. This the king did. He was at last showing signs of life again, but each day Farinelli had to rouse him. Every evening for almost ten years, he sang the same four arias, by composers long since forgotten, to raise the sovereign's spirits. The scores have been preserved; one is an imitation of a nightingale in love, a showpiece for castrati, replete with trills and embellishments. Farinelli was richly rewarded for his service and stayed on as a courtier, though it meant giving up his European career at the age of thirty-two—to serve in endless repetition as the nightingale of a bizarre Spanish court. The king remained strange and moody, and the court was a snakepit of intrigue, but the singer stayed, trusted, respected, and with many friends.

When Philip died and was succeeded by Ferdinand VI, Farinelli was free to expand his sphere of activity. He established an opera company that became famous throughout Europe; he trained singers, equipped theaters, and often acted as a diplomat, a mediator between the court and the government. His fame as a singer was matched by his reputation as a courtier; he was praised for his tact, amiability, and sincerity. He was involved in the building of a canal on the Tagus River. He bred Thoroughbreds and directed the opera and the royal chapel choir. He lured singers and set designers to Madrid for his opera; was knighted for his contributions to the wedding of the crown princess; had his portrait painted in the dress of a Spanish grandee. What Haydn's and Mozart's royal taskmasters denied them, Farinelli obtained with little effort.

Ferdinand died in 1759 and was succeeded by Charles III, who detested music and had no use for Farinelli. "I prefer my capons on my plate," Charles remarked when the most celebrated castrato of Europe came to pay his respects to the new king. Farinelli left for Italy with a broken heart and a royal pension, at the age of fifty-four; he withdrew to his villa near Bologna, among his memories and mementos. There he mourned for a quarter of a century, visited by kings, composers, prelates, and regents, a Narcissus contemplating his reflection in the past. The biggest celebrity in Bologna, Farinelli died there in 1782—the year Mozart decided against having a castrato sing the role of Osmin in his *Abduction from the Seraglio*. Opera as a vocal game, a vocal pyrotechnic display in costume, had had its day, and little Italian boys could sleep peacefully again.

CASTRATION, alas, has been a fact of life since the world began. Within the family of gods on Olympus, fathers, brothers, and sons emasculated each other. In antiquity, prisoners of war were castrated as a humiliation, and severed genitals served as trophies of victory. David, to prove his valor before being permitted to marry Saul's daughter, was told to bring back the genitals of a hundred Philistines. Zealous and in love, he slew twice that number and appropriated their private parts, thus providing Saul with proof that the Lord, who like the Americans does not like a loser, was with him. This Old Testament practice reappeared during colonial wars in Asia and Africa.

The Greeks and Romans, more practical, confined themselves to importing castrated slaves from distant lands. Sometimes these slaves enjoyed great esteem and trust in the aristocratic households that employed them, and, where the ladies were concerned, their misfortune was a virtue. The castrated slave as household pet of the well-to-do was fairly common until quite late in the Byzantine Empire. And from the household it was a small step, across the threshold of the Church, for the Byzantine rites to be embellished by the introduction of choral castrato singing.

The Church forbade castration, as we have said, but nevertheless was willing to tolerate castrati for the greater glory of God. Were not many other physical sacrifices made to this end, ranging from celibacy to self-flagellation to fasting? Did not theology instruct man to give up the baser instincts, below the belt, in pursuit of higher things? In certain sects, as well as in the case of Origenes, that unfortunate father of the Church, this led to self-castration, the sacrifice of one's manhood as the price of admission to the Kingdom of God.

The Italian practice of castrating young boys for artistic purposes was unique, however. The specter of poverty, especially in large families, must have been a strong argument for parents to acquiesce in this. According to one biography of Franz Joseph Haydn, he would have suffered the same fate if his father, the choirmaster of Saint Stephen's Cathedral in Vienna, had not intervened at the last minute. All things considered, the practice was probably more humane than putting unwanted children on doorsteps or sending them out to beg.

Little was known at the time about the biology of procreation. But, starting with Aristotle, who observed that the vocal cords relaxed when the weight of the testicles was removed, enough had been learned for the consequences of castration to be apparent. For a long time it was a tenet of psychiatry that rapists, child molesters, and homosexuals could be cured by castration—a onetime mutilation that, like an investment, would justify itself over time.

Almost all the castrati were "made in Italy," during the days when Italian opera and ecclesiastical singing were in full flower, when the choir school was as important as sport teams are today. The objective of the castrato singer was no different from that of his successor, the prima donna, which was to emerge from obscurity into the limelight with that one talent, the golden voice, and with it achieve great honor and fame. For most, it meant an arduous climb up the social ladder, and few reached the top. And there, whether it was in the Church or in opera, intrigue, scandal, and squabbling were the order of the day, not the maintaining of artistic standards.

The human voice, the soprano especially, elicits an emotional response stronger than does any other instrument, perhaps because of its fragile, personal quality, or perhaps as a matter of rapport. Music in itself has no specific meaning, but vocal music is based on words that, however inadequate they may be, join with the music to convey a message. In music, it is often difficult to separate the interpreter from the interpretation. Virtuoso pianists like Franz Liszt, Arthur Rubinstein, and Vladimir Horowitz were not only great performers but colorful personalities with wide cult followings. The same is true of singers; Caruso, Callas, and Luciano Pavarotti are familiar names even to those who hate music.

Where musical theater is concerned, however, there is something about the perfect soprano voice that can carry away the most rational and sedate of listeners, as I can personally attest. Frederica von Stade, a solitary figure in a velvet doublet, her hair hanging loose, stands on the stage of the Paris Opera as Cherubino, the enamored teenager in *Marriage of Figaro*, and sings the "Voi chè sapete." My soul dissolves, the audience thunders, the Chagall ceiling descends, and Mozart stirs in amazement in his wretched grave. Elisabeth Schwarzkopf, the betrayed, melancholy countess in a 1956 recording of *Figaro*, sings "Dovè sono," and no eye stays dry. How is it that Jessye Norman and Kiri Te Kanawa have achieved such eminence that they were invited to add luster to the two hundredth anniversary of the French Revolution and to a British royal wedding? Why do the Belgians riot when the Brussels opera gives a mediocre performance? There is substance and shadow in the singing human voice, argument and display. It is a form of communication that directly touches the human heart, and he who does not feel it is beyond redemption.

Contemporary Dutch composer Peter Schat once said that those who beat a path to the Amsterdam Concertgebouw for the Thursday evening concerts have not a soul but a little yellow balloon that becomes damp when it hears Brahms. Like Schat, I do not believe in the soul, but I do believe in that little yellow balloon, a hidden organ which begins to vibrate when it hears flawless soprano notes, and experiences a brief but unforgettable moment of pure joy. Miraculously, we can relive this experience through recordings; we can revisit the recent past by courtesy of a laser beam. This is a democratic luxury that no departed king, prelate, or Maecenas was able to enjoy. We, on the other hand, will never be able to appreciate the fascination of the castrato voice, with its seamless range and incredible virtuosity, its volume and power. We may listen to the music they sang, but it does not sound the same; the Italian way with the knife is gone. The Farinelli story is as sad as it is beguiling. For a time the voice was freed from its natural limits, but in the long run the price of two testicles for four octaves proved to be too high.

Extremes of Faith

Parthenogenesis

THE COMPARATIVE HISTORY of religions is based on the premise that nothing is sacred, and everything has happened before. That includes the birth of Christ to the Virgin Mary, an event celebrated by a dechristianized world at Christmas and which marks the beginning of our Western era. The new start for the recording of history was determined not by some meaningless calendar adjustment but by the incarnation of God.

Virgin birth is a common theme in ancient myths. Before God the Father, there was God the Mother, the earth goddess. In the Stone Age, when human life was short and full of uncertainty and infant mortality high, fertility was worshiped as the only defense against the ravages of existence: hence the few statuettes we have found are of female figures with pronounced sexual characteristics and bulging bellies.

The female sex hormone estrogen promotes the storage of fat in the breasts and on the hips, buttocks, and thighs. This body fat, which women now consider undesirable, is a source of energy essential to pregnancy and breast-feeding; it is also a factor governing fertility. A woman who is starving—by choice or otherwise, from anorexia or a lack of nourishment —becomes infertile. Her menstruation is irregular or ceases. If by chance a pregnancy occurs, she cannot nurse the child. The goddess of fertility's insatiable desire for fat is no mythological metamorphosis but a biological necessity.

It was only after the prehistoric nomads settled and man

as hunter or farmer began to assume a more defined role alongside the fertile mother that male gods began to appear —in the role of a child or a lover of the mother goddess. In Asia and the Middle East, the earliest worship was of the mother goddess, who brings the gift of life. From this come their prominent representations of the gateway to life, the mound of Venus and the labia majora.

In Greek mythology, the creation of the world out of chaos also begins with an earth mother, Gaea, who gives birth in her sleep to her son Uranus. As the ruler of heaven, Uranus impregnates her with rain and so causes the earth to flourish. Following a family quarrel, Gaea has Uranus castrated. It is only after the marriage of his brother and sister that Zeus is born. The birth supposedly took place on Crete, in a cave, where a goat cared for the baby. Tourists on donkeys can still reach this proto-Bethlehem, and parallels with the cave of the Nativity are inescapable.

Throughout classical mythology, miraculous births occur whenever the gods consort with mortals. Bacchus and Apollo resulted from Zeus's amorous travels, when he disguised himself as a man or bird in order to impregnate nymphs and the daughters of kings. Divine paternity implied virgin birth and gave the mortal offspring an aura of immortality. Their contemporaries believed that Alexander, Plato, and Pythagoras had come into the world by virgin birth, although the facts belied this. Heaven and earth unite, and a miracle is born.

Our era begins with the birth of Christ, and Western civilization—in spite of all resistance to the idea, in word and deed—remains a product of Christianity. The Church, Catholic or non-Catholic, has held to the virgin birth and worshiped, appealed to, and depicted the Virgin in a thousand ways. The symbol of womanhood, she has increasingly been venerated alongside the male Trinity, with as much if not greater fervor. The Virgin is a mythic figure in everyday life, the object of superstition and idolatry, but also an emblem of purity and compassion, an eternal fantasy. Her worship pervades our world and our era to an extent beyond anything humankind has ever experienced, projected as it is on a woman we know almost nothing about. She is a myth conjured out of thin air, made from the fabric of legend and cult, who grew in stature as the centuries passed.

THE PATH FROM BETHLEHEM to the universal Ave Maria was a long one. We find practically no mention of Mary in the earliest texts of the New Testament or in Paul's letters. In the Gospel of Saint Mark, the first of the four, Christ is unmindful of his mother and his brothers. The Gospel according to Saint Luke, written almost a century after the event, contains the full Christmas story, including the Annunciation, the visitation by the angel, and the Magnificat, and the crib and the shepherds. Here, Christ is born of a human being, not as a mythological act but in fulfillment of ancient prophesies and recurring messianic themes.

The last of the Gospels, that of Saint John, does not contain the Christmas story and describes Mary only as a distraught mother at the marriage feast in Cana and at the foot of the Cross. Only Saint Matthew, who sought to connect the Old Testament to the New, makes a clear though indirect allusion to Mary's virginity, in his reference to the prophet Isaiah's prediction that a maiden would become pregnant and bear a son whom men would call Emmanuel, "God with us." Matthew goes on to tell the story of the Immaculate Conception by intervention of the Holy Ghost, the birth of Christ, the flight to Egypt, and Herod's slaughter of the children, drawing a parallel with the child Moses, the savior of the Old Testament. Philologists now believe that Matthew, who used a Greek version of the Hebrew writings, was the victim of a translation error. The Greek word *parthenos*, "virgin," they say, is too restricted a rendering of the Hebrew word *alman*, "a young girl of marriageable age."

The virgin birth in the Gospels may have been an etymological misunderstanding, but in the Roman world it was accepted legend and denoted divine origin, and the Church Fathers had difficulty distinguishing the Christian myth from the heathen one. During the second century, they produced a new account of the event, based on an apocryphal gospel by Jacob, Christ's brother, which offered a detailed chronicle of the Holy Family. Though excluded from the Biblical canon, this account survived in varied forms, was embellished by other apocryphal stories, and found its way into the body of medieval legends. The Holy Family, in it, was more extensive than the one described by ecclesiastical dogma; Mary acquired parents, Joachim and Anna, who were revered as saints and whose relics were distributed throughout Europe. The spare narrative of the Gospels is here inflated into a sumptuous Oriental myth filled with elements of the Old Testament as well as heathen religions.

The myth of virgin birth was fueled by ignorance about the facts of procreation. Aristotle believed that women contained the substantive basis for life in their menstrual blood but that men had to provide that substance with form and animation. The male held the intangible spark; the female supplied the raw material. In the absence of a microscope, this opinion prevailed until the time of Harvey and Leeuwenhoek. It seemed entirely plausible, therefore, that the Holy Ghost, a life-endowing spirit, could cause the base substance in a female to assume shape and mobility. A deity switches on the human machine. Heaven's rain makes the earth yield fruit.

British historian Marina Warner has written a beautiful book about the veneration of Mary. Warner argues that the emergence of the Mary myth complemented the belief in the Resurrection. Born in a cave and wrapped in a cloth, Christ appeared to the world, and the virgin birth signified His divinity and immaculacy. Suffering the death of a criminal, wrapped in a shroud and buried in a cave, He would arise as the resurrected Savior.

The dedication of the sexual to the divine, the terrestrial to the celestial, figured also in the religions of antiquity. Ritual deflowering, temple prostitution, and virgin priestesses like Vesta and Pallas Athene of the Parthenon are examples of the merging of sacred and sexual. Christianity, in the person of Saint Augustine and the early Church Fathers, was the first religion to elevate virginity to the status of deliverance from sin. Mary became a second Eve, a primeval mother who obeyed God and did not pick the forbidden fruit that would drive her out of paradise.

Not far along in the history of the Church she dies and physically ascends to heaven, where she intercedes with God. She was prayed to and venerated, and the medieval Church built chapels for her and created her image as madonna, maid and mother of sorrows, queen of heaven, goddess of fertility, and patron saint of crusades and religious wars. She materialized in Lourdes and Fátima to deliver her messages—and to give millions of babies her name. Popular belief became unbending dogma when *she* was declared to have been conceived immaculately—that is, free of original sin. She became Joint Savior. Mary has been the inspiration for the most sublime creations of painters, sculptors, composers, and poets, and she is worshiped in the Eastern and even the Muslim world. An everlasting rosary has been established, of supplication to and adoration of Our Lady. The present pope demonstrates his piety by traveling to pray before her ebony-black effigy in Poland, putting all the troubles of the world in her care.

The Mary myth has another, more worldly aspect. It is the theological peg on which Christianity has hung its disdain for woman-as-man's-equal. There is no place for women in the Church. Subservient, the female is exhorted to bear children, even against her will, because that is her natural function. The only purpose her sexuality serves is procreation—the next best thing after virginity. Menstruation renders her impure. For these reasons, Mary is not the archetype of wife and mother but, rather, the symbol of a doctrine that says worldly life is sinful, sexuality is offensive, and all things feminine are to be despised. The world is full of guilt and transgression, which it cannot divest itself of except by renouncing biology—that is, itself.

So it was necessary for the Church to invent Mary, even if she never existed. The veneration of Mary is declining these days, and it appears likely that it will soon be limited to the credulous and the cultists—unless the Church can find a way to invest her constantly changing image with the attributes of First Feminist. For, besides inspiring profound devotion, she has been the cause of much guilt and despair: her virginal fertility rites an obstacle to every effort the world makes to achieve birth control. As the inequality between men and women diminishes, her role as compliant mother fades. Nor will there be much point for her to intercede in heaven, if it turns out that there is no one there. Her miracles and appearances will cause a stir only in the villages of southern Europe. The arts are seeking other female symbols, more variable and more worldly, and young people now flock to another Madonna.

VIRGIN BIRTH, or parthenogenesis, with which all Mariology begins, biologically antedates religious symbolism. It occurs in many insects, worms, and lizards, the latter being particularly instructive with regard to the male and female functions.

American biologists have studied several species of the whiptail lizard, including one species that consists of both males and females and another that has only females. The two species exhibit the same mating behavior, however. In the first case, the male lizard licks the female, mounts her, and brings their external sexual organs into contact. In the unisexual species, the lizards, even though genetically female, are able to behave as males, because acts of courtship and mating are necessary to the reproductive process. Hormones induce the ripening of the ovum, and male behavior stimulates their secretion. In the first half of the cycle, the ovum is affected by the female hormone estrogen. When the ovum is ready for fertilization, the estrogen level drops and the level of progesterone, the hormone that ensures the permeability of the ovum, rises. The unisexual lizards exhibit male behavior only during this second phase of the cycle. The reason: their progesterone is stored in receptors in the anterior hypothalamus of the brainstem. The brain, human or animal, is bisexual. It has separate circuits of nerve cells and receptors. The male hormones, which induce male behavior, are stored in the anterior hypothalamus; the female hormones are stored in the posterior nucleus. What circuit will be used in the embryo and in later stages of life depends on the genetic gender; the male fetus produces male hormones, the female fetus does not.

Unisexual lizards possess the same dual neural circuits as

their genetic ancestors. Though genetically female, they can utilize the male circuit by making their male receptors store the female hormone progesterone. Thus, without the benefit of a male or any male hormones, the female lizard, exhibiting female behavior during the first half of her cycle and male behavior during the second half, makes pseudocopulation possible. This pseudocopulation in turn causes the ripening of the ovum, which divides without any contact with male sperm. And so nature here manages without fertilization, and the female lizard, by activating a dormant male circuit in her brain, can be self-sufficient.

Nature makes male and female biologically equal, mutually dependent and complementary, even when procreation is possible by substituting the presence of a male with male behavior—at least in the case of whiptail lizards. Mythology, on the other hand, is concerned with a different reality, one that is invented, idealized, and personified. In this sense, Mary is truly a handmaiden not of the Lord but of Christian theology. Only casually mentioned in the Bible, she was enlarged because the Church Fathers needed her to convince Jew, Greek, and heathen of the divine and human nature of her Son. In Mary's person, the worldly became celestial, the defiled pure, and sexual indulgence the sinful opposite of virgin birth. The transience of life—the subject of Goethe's *Faust* and Mahler's Eighth Symphony—was more apparent than real. The enormities and imperfections of mankind could be redeemed by the eternal feminine.

In our Western culture, this is the task Mary has performed. She has been celebrated on canvas and in music, and venerated as maid and mother, queen of heaven, handmaiden and savior, the constantly changing symbol of a Christian, and largely male, conceit that seeks to trade the world for Heaven and a sordid existence for an unblemished eternity. The Virgin Mary is the metaphor for this barter.

The mythological concept of the female has lately come to represent the denigration and suppression of women in the real world. But this idea, too, is on the wane. Other goddesses, including those of the stage, the silver screen, and popular music, have taken over, ranging from Madonna to Mother Teresa, from Madame Curie to Marilyn Monroe. In a diverse society not bound by religious symbolism, each person chooses for himself—rather than let God choose for him—an image of the eternal feminine. We continue to look up in wonder, like lizards in the sun.

Heretics

HERETICS ARE THOSE who deviate from orthodox Christian doctrine and therefore must be converted, excommunicated, or persecuted. A clear enough definition—but what is this orthodox doctrine, and why does a person deviate from it? Why is he willing to be hounded to death, even suffer martyrdom, for a belief? The Dutch word for heretic, *ketter*, comes from Cathar, which comes from the Greek word *katharos*, "pure one." Catharism, active in the south of France, was the first important heretical movement of the Middle Ages. It lasted less than a hundred years, but is a textbook example of heresy and its suppression.

At one time, the Christians themselves were heretics and persecuted, in the Roman Empire. Then, under Emperor Constantine, Church and state fell into each other's arms, and whoever deviated from the holy creed after that could be sure not only of condemnation by the Church but also of persecution by the state. The persecuted became the persecutors, and the Church Father Saint Augustine was the first inquisitor, his *civitas dei* having many of the characteristics of a dictatorship. The Christian doctrine was totalitarian: it offered salvation, through the grace of God, to sinful, evil humanity—a way out of this vale of tears—and it was the Christian state's responsibility that all who deviated from that way were tracked down and either forced to recant or cast out. With Augustine, the light of the classical world dimmed and the darkness of the

Middle Ages descended—the Christian empire, one God and one Church, with a monopoly on the truth.

The new Christian Church had to contend with many heresies, ranging from differences in creed to heathen influences, heresies having a variety of social consequences. But with the gradual emergence of orthodoxy, a church community, and organized religious instruction, the heresies seemed to disappear. Those that did occur during the early Middle Ages often involved only individuals and were more likely to be tolerated than suppressed. Only after the year 1000 did heresies reappear in any number. Because of the unrest they caused, these tended to provoke secular as well as ecclesiastical reaction. By now the Church had great power in the society, and as a result of its collaboration with the secular authorities its religious values had become obscured by cupidity, wealth, and politics. In protest, small groups of an anticlerical persuasion began to form in western Europe.

The Cathars were different from these, however. Their heresy stemmed from a deep-seated belief that was not even of Christian origin—the Persian doctrine of Manichaeanism (to which Augustine himself had adhered at one time). This doctrine involved two active principles, good and evil. Evil consisted of all material, physical things, and the world was Satan's empire. Man was a stranger on this earth, and his only treasure was his soul, which had to escape its prison of a mortal body and seek, through many reincarnations, to return to the kingdom of the spirit and God. Visible reality was temporary and ruled by evil; the true reality was that which man could not perceive.

The Catharist doctrine had arisen earlier in Bulgaria, in the Rhineland, and in northern Italy, but its full flowering came in the region of Languedoc in southwestern France, in the middle of the twelfth century. A prosperous area, carrying on an extensive trade with the Middle East; and an open society, with its own language, the *langue d'Oc*, and troubadours and poetry and the flourishing cities of Carcassonne and Toulouse, all under the benign rule of the counts of Toulouse. The French kings had no hold on Languedoc, and the Church there was in serious decline. The new Catharist religion first attracted simple folk, later people of prominence.

The Cathars were pacifist and temperate, and they treated men and women equally. They had no hierarchy, no desire for possessions or authority, and they withdrew from the world the Church had tried to dominate. Living according to their convictions, they rejected the Church and all religious services. The one sacramental act they recognized was the *consolamentum*. Ordinary believers could not receive the rite unless they were on their deathbeds. A handful of "perfect ones," the *bonshommes*, who lived in strict abstinence and had forsaken the world, were granted the *consolamentum*, or soothing benediction, and these were the spiritual leaders. The *bonshommes* moved through the towns and countryside preaching and extending the *consolamentum*, and won respect for their modest and worthy way of life. On foot or on muleback, they managed to cover the entire south of France. They came from all levels of society, and some, though they had little education, gained great renown for their eloquence. The prime example was Guilhebert de Castres, who traveled around for thirty years and was highly regarded in many regions.

Initially the Church did little to stop the heresy, although she was uneasy, and the counts of Toulouse were reluctant to take action against so large a group of their own subjects. The first move came when a youthful new pope, Innocent III, ascended the throne of Saint Peter in 1198. He appointed papal delegates, who were to report directly to him, and sent them to Languedoc with instructions to restore the faith by sermons, conversions, and admonitions to the heretics and local prelates. Some delegates appealed to the secular authorities to bring the heretics to heel by force—in vain. In the summer of 1206, a Spanish cleric, Domingo de Guzmán, crossed the Pyrenees with his bishop and heard about the discouraging results of the papal delegates. Domingo attributed their lack of success to their imperious manner and ostentation. He advised them to travel the country, living as simply as their adversaries did, and preaching the true faith. He set an example himself by devoting nine years to disputations and sermons against the *bonshommes*. He became the founder of the Dominican order, the friar-preachers of the Church.

In 1207, a public debate took place, in the castle of Montreal, between the papal delegates, including Domingo, and the Catharist preachers, including Guilhebert de Castres. In accordance with the rules of such theological tournaments, there were referees, umpires, and an audience. The debate lasted two weeks and was conducted in the vernacular. It is claimed that as a result of the Church's convincing arguments, 150 heretics recanted. The arguments were recorded for later study by the adversaries.

The umpires were unable to decide who won, so a sign from God had to be invoked. Domingo's testament of faith was cast into the fire but it did not burn; it rose up from the flames unscathed and left a scorch mark on one of the castle beams. (The beam can be seen today in the nearby church of Fanjeaux.) The adversaries' documents were consumed by the fire. In a few years, the followers of Domingo would consign the Cathars themselves to the flames. When books are burned, the burning of people soon follows. The miracle of that trial by fire must have made an impression, for two hundred years later Fra Angelico, Dominican painter and monk, immortalized it beautifully.

After the debate of Montreal, little happened. One of the papal delegates, an advocate of force against the heretics, was murdered, possibly at the behest of the count of Toulouse. Pope Innocent, wanting retribution, ordered his delegates to assemble the secular authorities for a crusade against the heretics. The count of Toulouse, after doing penance by being whipped naked, was allowed to pa..icipate. In the summer of 1209, an army of knights, bishops, hirelings, and adventurers crossed the Rhône to compel Languedoc's submission to the Church.

A chapter of French history that was kept under wraps for a long time now unfolded—the genocide of a people and a culture, organized by the Church. It had far-reaching consequences for the history of Europe. The first city taken was Béziers, and all its inhabitants, numbering some thirty thousand, were slaughtered, nine thousand of them in the church. Carcassonne was the next to fall. Then smaller cities and citadels were besieged and invaded, under the leadership of one Simon de Montfort. This merciless campaigner died during the siege of Toulouse, his head smashed by a stone from a catapult aimed by a Cathar woman. Innocent also died about this time, and the violence abated temporarily.

A second crusade was launched a few years later, this time with the support of the French king, who hoped to extend his domain. The nobility of Languedoc, led by the count of Toulouse, acquiesced, and a council convened in Toulouse to organize the persecution of the heresy in the territories already subdued.

The Inquisition began in 1233, during an interval of peace.

The new pope, Gregory IX, charged the Dominicans with carrying out the persecution of the heretics, without the possibility of appeal and beyond the jurisdiction of the local clergy. Peace held greater menace for the Cathars than had the fighting of both crusades. No longer able to profess their faith openly, they went into hiding or retreated to impregnable fortresses like the mountain fastness of Montségur, where heretical noblemen and a sympathetic populace protected them. The count of Toulouse's new position of neutrality was of little help to the Inquisition.

In cities and towns, meanwhile, heretics were flushed out or betrayed and turned over to the Inquisition, which then prepared a formal accusation. The ensuing investigation took place in secret, and a rumor was sufficient justification for an indictment. Guilt was predetermined; the only way to save one's life was to recant and atone. Evidence was obtained by deception and torture, and the suspect had no rights whatsoever. The Church, officially opposed to torture as being incompatible with the Christian ethic, did not mind leaving that matter to the temporal authorities, as well as the carrying out of the sentence, death at the stake. The Inquisition required the public execution of heretics in order to sustain its reign of terror. Even heretics who had died natural deaths were disinterred so they could be burned. Greater weight, however, was given to recantation, conversion, and penance, as visible triumphs of the Church over deviation. Those doing penance lost their property, were scourged, and sent on crusades. They also had to wear for many years, at home and in public, an outer sign of their sinfulness which Domingo devised—a large yellow cross on chest and back, a precursor of the Star of David worn by Jews under the Nazis. The *bonshommes* had to stitch a third cross to their caps.

What we know of those early heretics and their fate we owe to their persecutors, who maintained meticulous written records. The French historian Le Roy Ladurie drew his description of events in his hometown of Mountaillou from the records of the Inquisition kept by the local bishop—who rose to become pope after exterminating the last of the Cathars.

Resistance to the Inquisition of the Dominicans followed. Members of one of the more notorious courts, stopping overnight in a castle while traveling, were murdered by a group from Montségur. The aristocracy and the people continued to secede from king and Church, but were ruthlessly brought to heel. All that remained were a few Catharist strongholds, called "synagogues of Satan," in the barren mountain landscape at the foot of the Pyrenees. The castle of Montségur was the most important. Knights, squires, "perfect ones," and simple believers had sought refuge there, five hundred fugitives. The bald mountain is still an impressive sight today, a limestone outcrop in the middle of the landscape, crowned with the long, shiplike castle ruin.

The third and last crusade against the remaining Cathars started in the summer of 1243, led by the archbishop of Narbonne. The steep, forbidding slopes leading to Montségur did not favor a siege, and the stronghold was provisioned at night by means of hidden pathways. Early the next year, however, the assailants managed to secure a vantage point immediately below the fortress and were able to batter the walls of the castle with their catapults. The beleaguered Cathars finally surrendered, knowing that the stake awaited all who had been or still were heretics, and all who had received the *consolamentum* during the siege.

On a single day in March 1244, as many as 210 people were burned alive on a giant pyre at the foot of the mountain.

Led by their "perfect ones," men, women, and children went to meet the flames; their cremation, inside a stockade of straw and branches, was supervised by the inquisitor. This marked the end of the heresy and the end also of the culture and language of Languedoc, which became crown land. Although a few other hiding places of the heresy remained to be discovered and destroyed, the Masada of the Cathars had been taken.

Their memory is kept alive at the scene of the massacre, as well as at other Catharist strongholds, where similar massacres occurred. Like the Basques and the Bretons, today's inhabitants of Languedoc retain a longing for their former language, their roots. They are French more by necessity than by choice.

What was the reason for the sad fate of this odd heresy of long ago? It was the first popular heresy of any consequence, and it was stamped out within a hundred years by the joint effort of temporal and ecclesiastical powers. The Church needed a legal justification for its action; three crusades and an Inquisition directed against the people of one's own country were unheard of. Not that tolerance was a prime Christian virtue at the time, for those who knew the way to heaven wanted to point everyone else in the right direction, if necessary by force. The restoration in 1200 of an ecclesiastical hierarchy under papal authority and with political alliances had strengthened the long arm of the Church, although it also had aroused disgust at the arrogance and lavish life-style of the clergy. Still, there had to be a better reason for the persecution of the heretics than ecclesiastical unification. The justification came from the image the Cathars themselves provided. They were different, different in their beliefs and their way of life, and that made them a threat to Church and state. They were also strong in number and might have become a menace had preventive action not been taken.

Thus the heretic became the scapegoat for various misfortunes. He was accused of secret and bloody rituals; was made an object of suspicion, with no way to defend himself; was forced to return to the Church or be cast out into darkness. His extermination was legitimized in the mock trials of the Inquisition, which would not have been possible without the development of a social order in the cities, the emergence of a literate class, and the influence of the monasteries. Historical parallels are risky, but might not the Nuremberg Tribunal have condemned the murder of the Cathars as genocide, and the Dominican order as a criminal organization? Indeed, according to English historian R. J. Moore, Europe after the year 1000 dedicated itself to the persecution of the defenseless. The first to suffer were the Cathars; after the great crusades, Jews became the victims, but lepers and whores also were hunted down and expelled. Then came "witches," Protestants, freethinkers, and Baptists—until colonization, the slave trade, and war opened up other avenues for persecution.

The Inquisition led not only to the extermination of the Cathars in France but to the expulsion of the Jews and Moors from Spain, and to the crushing of Protestantism in Italy. To this end, it was necessary to demonize the heretic, whether Jew or leper, to accuse him of secret rites, orgies, child sacrifice, and the worship of Satan. To justify the violence, the danger to the Church was exaggerated and the number of heretics inflated. And the Church had to seem to be mankind's sole salvation.

English historian Norman Cohn, in his extensive and detailed 1975 study of the European witch-hunts of the fifteenth and sixteenth centuries, showed that there had been no basis in fact for the hysteria. The "witches," like the Jews, heretics, or lepers of other times, were the projection of the fantasies, myths, and obsessions of a society—"Europe's inner demons," to quote the title Cohn gave his book. The allegations of infanticide and cannibalism, of orgies and devil worship, were the reverse side of a rigid religion that gave the spirit precedence over the flesh, the commandments over freedom of action, detachment over emotion. The complete hold Christianity had on this society provoked a malevolent and bestial reaction, a collective delusion that transformed others into purveyors of evil. The inner demons were projected onto Cathars, Moors, or Jews, and these children of Satan had to repent or pay the price.

The Inquisition disappeared when the Church lost her supremacy after the Reformation, when excommunication ceased to have meaning for the rationalists and agnostics of the Enlightenment. Even the name was dropped at the beginning of this century. By then the dreaded Inquisition had become a paper tiger whose sole function was to place books on the Index and make many a Catholic theologian's life miserable. The odor of the pyre had disappeared centuries before, but the European demons of obsession and delusion, baptized Catholic, did not remain Catholic. The Holocaust occurred, and was tolerated by an enlightened and dechristianized Europe. And, like Pilate, governments and churches washed their hands in innocence. New crusades were undertaken to such realms of evil as Vietnam. South American and South African death squads disposed of those who would not submit to the authority of the state.

New minorities, ranging from immigrants to homosexuals, are denounced as sources of crime and disease, and their differentness is made out to be a menace. The history of the

West would appear to be a liberal one, a struggle for freedom of thought and religious belief and way of life, for the right of the individual to self-determination. But it has also been a history of collective paranoia toward anyone who is different, a history full of *apartheid* and persecution. This may be due less to Western culture than to human nature, the universal desire to bring human sacrifices to one's gods. Cain the farmer kills Abel the shepherd, whose sacrifice to the Lord had been more acceptable than his own, and a quarter of the existing population then dies in an orgy of religious malice and fanaticism. Abraham is willing to sacrifice his son. The Jewish elders want Christ put to death rather than risk having their people misled by a charlatan. Greek mythology is replete with gods who devour mortals. The Aztecs ritually pluck out the hearts of their young men.

The Church burns witches and heretics; the state regards the sacrifice of its citizens in war as manure on the acres of the future. The one true faith claims more victims than do oil or gold. When one man sees another not as a wolf but as a sacrificial lamb, the altars are aflame.

Anorexia Religiosa

ACCORDING TO the Book of Genesis, God created man in His image, and Adam and Eve strolled in naked perfection among the animals in the Garden of Eden. Then they ate the forbidden apple and became aware of good and evil, guilt and mortality. They covered their nakedness with fig leaves and fled from paradise, ashamed of their bodies and the parts thereof. A few chapters later, Noah drank too much of the harvest of his vineyard and lay naked in his tent. One of his sons laughed at him; the other two, walking backward, drew a blanket over their drunken father to avoid seeing his nakedness. Sober again, Noah praised the two sons and cursed the one who had laughed.

In Genesis the human body is no longer innocent perfection, the crown of Creation, but a cause of sweat and tears, a cause for shame. Since then, the symbolic significance of the body has undergone many transformations. The female form became the symbol of such abstract virtues as freedom, justice, and wisdom, from the Parthenon to the statue in New York Harbor that was the first sight of America for millions of immigrants. The female form, adorned or stylized, represents the Muses, the Madonna, and the Sirens—art, redemption, seduction. The Republic of the Seven United Netherlands and the Mother of God are similarly portrayed as virgins: pure and gently encircled by roses, defenseless symbols of another reality. The female form, veiled and draped to suggest motherhood or virginity, has greater symbolic power than the male body. Fashion, according to anthropologists, is a game with sexual undertones, and women are better endowed for it. But the male domination of Western culture (aside from the homoeroticism of some classical sculpture) has imposed itself as well on the female body, has made it conform to male ideas. The human shape provided by the Creator falls short of the mark; it needs improvement, in an endless variety of ways. The art of painting begins with the primitive daubing of the body; the earliest sculpture is of genitalia. Obesity becomes a sign of wealth, body hair an embellishment, and if nature proves inadequate, wigs, corsets, shoes, uniforms, and jewelry come to the rescue. In this the Russian general is no different from the New York photographer's model, although the images they seek to project are not the same. The poorest nomads of southern Africa, the Bushmen, may roam naked through the Kalahari Desert, but their women sport the epitome of pulchritude, an enormous accumulation of fat in the buttocks. It is both an ornament and a source of energy, like the hump of the camel. By manipulation, these women also stretch their external genitalia into a sort of apron. The early Dutch colonists considered them animals and sometimes sent them to Europe as circus curiosities. One such unfortunate was Saartje Baartman, "the Hottentot Venus," who was exhibited as a freak in England and France. After her death, the famous biologist Baron Georges Cuvier performed an autopsy on the lower half of her body. The mysterious apron, he found, consisted of two labia minora stretched to their limits. These genitalia are still preserved in a jar in the basement of the Musée de l'Homme in Paris.

The female form has a natural history determined by heredity, nutrition, occupation, and procreation. It also has an unnatural history, involving manipulation, fashion, sexual repression, mutilation, and distortion. Today's tall, slender, tanned women are no less an exaggeration than the pale, plump, curvaceous women of Rubens and Rembrandt.

A contemporary allegory of the female form can be drawn from the clinical picture of anorexia nervosa. This is an affliction that occurs mainly, but not exclusively, in young girls during puberty. Its frequency seems to be increasing at a considerable rate. Unless it is only our fascination with the phenomenon that is growing. But reliable statistics from English girls' schools and American ballet studios indicate that the increase is real. And it is particularly noticeable in upper social levels. The complaint is classified as a dietary disorder, but this self-imposed starvation is a means rather than an end. Severe weight loss results from the burning up of body fat. Warnings, threats, and rewards have little effect on the sufferer; it is the growing thinner that provides the greatest reward, the achievement of the lowest weight possible. Sooner or later, physical side effects become apparent. Menstruation is delayed, the hair changes, the heartbeat slows, and, in spite of enervation, episodes of intense activity occur, sometimes alternating with episodes of gluttony and self-induced vomiting. In its most severe form, anorexia nervosa is life threatening, because with it a simple infection can prove fatal.

The disorder normally begins at puberty, disguised as a slimming diet along with a regimen of exercise—an ostensibly healthy change in habits, a change millions of young women vainly swear to make. The usual goal: to look like someone who is thinner, to avoid being ridiculed as overweight. Sometimes the change is triggered by a traumatic event: a serious illness, the loss of a friend or family member, even a school exam. Conflicts with parents are also cited, but they are so common during puberty that they cannot be pinpointed as a factor.

The young woman's weight falls below 90 pounds; her physical condition and appearance deteriorate, to the consternation of those around her, who do what they can to coax her to eat. She loses interest in her surroundings, shuns personal contact, sleeps badly, feels cold, and concentrates on just one thing—not eating. She denies having a weight problem but continues to diet; no matter what the scale says, she is too fat. She wants to demonstrate her willpower; she must reach the weight she has set her heart on. Her obsession with eating increases, and her starved body is still too fat, because her target weight is continually lowered. The hormones that govern the menstrual cycle, produced by the frontal lobe of the pituitary gland, decrease in concentration in the blood. This symptom is usually secondary to the starvation itself. It also occurs in cases of forcible starvation. So it seems unlikely, though so far there is no proof either way, that anorexia is the result of an endocrine disorder.

Explanations of anorexic behavior vary with the perspective of the observer, and they tend to conflict. The clinical picture is not new. It was described in detail almost a century ago by clinicians in England and France, when a large number of cases of what was called anorexia hysterica were diagnosed. Troubled family relationships seemed to be a precondition then, and the celebrated French neurosurgeon Jean-Martin Charcot believed that isolation and a strict regimen were the most promising treatment. For him, it was a simple matter of who dictated the eating habits. And those hysterical, debilitated girls, in an advanced stage of anorexia, apparently were no match for the authoritarian professor; they submitted to whatever he prescribed. Hysteria, an unspecific concept these days, was a diagnosis that came easily to neurosurgeons then.

Of all the patients whose analyses Freud so exhaustively documented, only two, Anna and Emma, suffered from eating disorders in addition to their other abnormalities. Freud, who had spent some months working in Charcot's clinic, concluded that anorexia was due to an emotional disturbance. Aversion to food, he believed, was linked to the fear of one's own sexuality, the result of a hidden childhood trauma.

French psychiatrist Pierre Janet, a contemporary of Freud, noted the uncontrollable desire to lose weight, but he was also struck by the euphoria and other physical manifestations of the disorder, a sort of heightened consciousness combined with the suppression of such sensations as hunger or sexual desire —as though anorexia had some deeper cause. Further research into the psychogenesis of anorexia was stopped for a generation by the advent of somatic medicine. Then an emaciated young woman died after becoming pregnant, and a famous endocrinologist discovered abnormalities in her pituitary gland. A hormonal disorder seemed a likely explanation—until it became clear that emaciation in women after they gave birth was usually due to a pituitary gland weakened by the pregnancy and then damaged by excessive loss of blood. This "Simmonds' syndrome" was obviously something other than anorexia nervosa.

The search for the cause of anorexia nervosa has now shifted from patient to environment. Authority conflicts with parents, the urge to conform to an ideal of slenderness dictated by fashion, the search for personal identity in the context of a strict home and school, all these have been examined as elements in the basic conflict—the struggle for independence being the end and self-starvation the means. A rite of passage from obedient child to adult woman. An intensively felt and ritually demonstrated desire to escape the gilded cage of her surroundings.

Psychotherapists R. Van Deth and Walter Vandereycken, in their fascinating historical survey of anorexia nervosa, point to a number of factors that might have a bearing on the increasing frequency of the disorder over the last hundred years. For example, the frustration of an ambitious family, with high educational goals for its children, when confronted by a rebellious daughter during the crisis of puberty. They believe that certain cultural developments, like earlier sexual maturation, greater freedom for young people to choose roles and patterns of behavior, and the changing ideal of the perfect feminine form, have added to a woman's uncertainty at a time when she is trying to gain control of her life. In their view, eating disorders are manifestations of this struggle.

This sounds plausible enough—but is it the whole explanation? In almost every phase of their lives, Western women are concerned about their weight and their appearance, and constantly resort to diets of all descriptions, and to exercise, and to pills. The problem: there is always so much food within reach, so many snacks! But this hardly applies to those young girls in their prime who are starving themselves, often over many years and at the risk of permanent damage to their health. The syndrome remains an enigma, and no therapy—other than forced feeding—has much effect. The therapist can do little more than offer patience and understanding to the young woman on her mysterious detour, until at some point she decides to return to the main road.

ANOREXIA NERVOSA may seem to be limited to the Western cultural context of the bourgeois family, the education ethic, the crisis of puberty, the daily battlefield of the dinner table, where the refusal to eat is the young girl's weapon. In fact, this strategy is not the sole property of twentieth-century female teenagers in prosperous countries. Abstinence from food has a far more extensive history and a far broader significance. The hunger strike can be a political tool, to attract public attention; it has been employed by Gandhi in India, by Irish terrorists, by West German terrorists, by British suffragettes, and by South African political prisoners. The pressure is obvious—if the authorities do not give in, the hunger striker will die. His blood will be on their hands. Starvation as protest is quite different from anorexia nervosa; it is an action calculated for the effect on others, for publicity, for the admiration and perhaps personal gain to be derived.

Fasting, another form of self-starvation, is a religious practice as old as Western civilization. It is considered a means of purification, because demonic forces can defile the body through food. According to the Christian tradition of abstinence and atonement, the human body is a cage in which the soul, aspiring to heaven, is held fast. Through asceticism and self-discipline, the urges of the flesh can be brought under control, and in this state of spirituality one can come closer to God. After the reign of Emperor Constantine, when Christianity became the state religion, the persecution and martyrdom of Christians ended. So a new form of penitence came to be practiced among holy men, who banished themselves to precarious and solitary lives in the wilderness. A similar asceticism did not come into vogue again until the late Middle Ages, with its dread of the devil and hell, its plagues and wars. Johan Huizinga, in his *Waning of the Middle Ages*, describes the overheated atmosphere of a daily life permeated by religion. What was thought sublime then verges on the ridiculous now. Elements of heathen belief mingled with each mystery, and faith and superstition were often indistinguishable. Every action, however commonplace, was charged with religious significance; every ritual was a symbol of or reference to Christ. Religious ardor, like the whole of medieval society, was characterized by stark contrasts, by unbridled ecstasy and profound penitence. The latter included not only the fasting of ascetics, mystics, and holy men, but also flagellation, sleeping on beds of nails, and other varieties of self-mortification, in imitation of the Passion of Christ. Some holy men are rumored to have subsisted solely on eucharistic wafers. Such extreme asceticism, in a world in which so many struggled constantly to obtain food, must have greatly impressed the community.

American historian R. M. Bell, a student of the relationship between society and its saints, speculates about whether the fasting practices of the Middle Ages had anything in common with anorexia nervosa. Since the year 1200, the Catholic Church has proclaimed 261 Italian women to be blessed, venerable, or servants of God. One third of them have left too few biographical details for anything to be said about them. Of the remaining 170, it appears that fully one half suffered from some form of anorexia. For a few dozen, because they are famous or notorious, the evidence is clear. Bell chose a number of saints of the late Middle Ages from Tuscany and Umbria as examples of the clinical picture of religious anorexia, and compared them with the anorexia of today. In spite of the intervening centuries, there seem to be great similarities between these two forms of extreme behavior.

Research into the psychopathology of a saint's life is not easy. The biography was usually compiled by admirers at a time when his saintliness was taken for granted. The stories are essentially the same. What matters is not the facts but the saintly example that has been set. The facts are presented faithfully enough, but their purpose is to inspire not the historian or psychiatrist but the believer. The psychiatrist lacks another essential—direct contact with the patient. Thus all psychobiography is at the very best secondhand and unverifiable. Freud put Leonardo da Vinci on his couch, that procrustean bed of psychoanalysis, but he could not explain Leonardo's genius.

Nor is it easy to understand the saint in the context of his time and in the light of a religious, personal experience different from any we can now imagine. Another problem—the most intractable—is that religious and medical explanations rarely complement or shed light on each other. Joan of Arc's voices become no easier to understand when they are attributed to schizophrenia, and it does not help much to describe the visions of Teresa of Avila as hysteria. Saintliness constitutes an exception to the rules of everyday behavior and experience. Shunning human contact, saints concentrate on achieving perfection in the sight of God. In most cases, their role of setting an example renders a historical approach difficult and a medical one meaningless. The fact that some saints strike us today as bizarre, fanatic, mentally disturbed, or unbelievable is irrelevant. They fulfilled their destinies during their lifetimes, and what remains is relics and legends.

Without question, one of the most intriguing and most celebrated of the saints was Catherine of Siena, the patron saint of Italy and a highly influential spiritual leader of the late Middle Ages. Catherine was the next to last of twenty-three children, several of whom died young. She was raised in a family of weavers in Siena, a prosperous city that still retains its Gothic character and atmosphere of mystery. Her birth occurred shortly before the great plague of 1348, which took two thirds of the people of Siena to their graves. The Black Death was seen as God's punishment for the people's moral corruption. Anxiety, guilt, and repentance pervaded the city, and penitential sermonizers and flagellants announced the judgment of the Almighty. As religious fervor and devotion mounted, however, so did discord and decadence in the ranks of the Church.

Catherine grew up in a traditional family and was, of course, expected to marry. At an early age, she had visions and, secretly and repeatedly, beat herself with a whip. At the age of fifteen, against the wishes of her parents and after the death of an adored older sister, she shut herself off from the world. She refused to marry, resolving to remain a virgin and belong to God; she cut off her hair; she devoted herself to meditation and nocturnal vigils. She ate only bread and raw vegetables, drank only water, and bound herself with chains, and never spoke except at confession. She whipped herself until she bled, and lost half her body weight. Her parents did everything they could to get her to change her ways, but eventually she left home to join a lay order of Dominicans. There, in the company of widows and virgins, she performed good works and entreated the Lord to let her atone for her family's failure to understand.

The story of her life is based on the work of her last father confessor, Raymond of Capua, later a general in the Dominican Order. After her death—like Christ, she was thirty-three—he tried to reconstruct her story from eyewitness accounts and her letters. Unable to write, she had dictated hundreds of letters, and her admonishments went to popes, monarchs, and prelates throughout Europe.

From her eighteenth to her twenty-eighth year Catherine lived and worked in Siena, a famished young woman who spent her days in prayer, self-chastisement, and the nursing of the sick. Her piety attracted disciples from well-to-do families; they assisted her and later accompanied her on her travels. Her obsession with God—her theopathy—revealed itself in visible ways. After receiving communion, she fell into a trance, and the five stigmata, the wounds of Christ, appeared on her hands, feet, and chest. God spoke directly to her in such trances, which were states of spiritual exaltation that followed extreme physical exhaustion from lack of food and sleep. She vomited up all food that was not raw vegetables. She cared for vagabonds, prisoners, and lepers, and did not shrink from the most repellent tasks.

Her union with God was not only spiritual; it was physical, too. She wore a wedding ring (invisible to others) made from the foreskin of the circumcised Christ, and her marriage had been consecrated by the Holy Mother in the presence of the apostles and saints. In emulation of Christ's agony, she sucked pus from the wounds of her patients and beat herself until she bled. The intensity of her suffering was eased by the reunion of her soul with Christ in a transport of erotic ecstasy. People sought her out because of her visions and transports and because she appeared to exemplify the will of God. Her excesses also elicited some disbelief and criticism, but that only added to her fame as an emissary of God.

Catherine's uncompromising renunciation of everything physical and worldly was in stark contrast to the lives of those who ruled her church. Pope Clement, a Frenchman, because he kept a mistress, and because of political unrest, had left Rome and moved to Avignon at the beginning of the terrible fourteenth century. There, one after another, seven French popes and their cardinals had been offering their wares for sale. Positions, dispensations, indulgences, and relics were all to be had for hard cash. The papal court lived in unimaginable excess. Corruption was rife from top to bottom, with threats of anathema and excommunication used to compel payment. Priests lived with women, extorted money, and were barely capable of fulfilling their religious functions. Forgiveness and penance could be bought, and the last remnants of piety had been replaced by usury and vice. In the whole *Decameron* of Boccaccio, Catherine's contemporary and fellow Tuscan, there is not one cleric who is not a rogue, a swindler, or a womanizer.

The Church, Christ's bride, was flaunting a very worldly body. Catherine, believing herself not only the symbolic but the actual bride of Christ, rejected that body.

In the five years preceding her death, the emaciated and reclusive Catherine chose to involve herself in European politics. Accompanied by a few followers, she traveled to Avignon, where Pope Gregory XI was reigning under French suzerainty. With all the force she could muster, she appealed to the pope to return to Rome, reform the Church, and initiate a crusade against the Turks. Removed from their religious packaging, these were extremely practical pieces of advice. The pope's association with the king of France diminished his spiritual authority. In the words of Petrarch, who was living there, Avignon was a sewer where the filth of the universe gathered. Also, it would be better if the mercenary troops then ravaging Europe were let loose upon the Turks instead. Catherine's repeated pleas—she knew she was speaking for God—persuaded the pope to abandon the Rhône for the Tiber in 1377, but he died a year later.

His successor, Urban VI, an arrogant and tactless man, soon locked horns with the princes and the cardinals. As his predecessor had done, he gave an audience to Catherine (her father confessor had to interpret her Tuscan dialect). She dictated countless letters to the pope and to the royal houses, begging for reform of the Church, which seemed to be sinking deeper into a morass of scandal and political dissent. Finally the cardinals, tired of Rome and Urban, declared that the change of residence had been illegal, moved back to Avignon, and elected a counterpope—a character every bit as nasty as Urban. The era of the Great Schism, of popes and counter-popes, murder and mayhem, divide and conquer, had begun.

Feeling cruelly deceived by the pope and his cardinals—the shepherds she had thought to restore to their flock in Rome—Catherine retreated from the violence. She was tormented by guilt about the part she had played in the pope's return to Rome and was in agonies of doubt as to whether she had indeed been carrying out God's will.

At the beginning of the year of her death, 1380, during a fast, she also stopped drinking water. In a few weeks, as a result of dehydration, she collapsed. The euphoria and animation typical of anorexia had given way to resignation and a yearning for death. She lived on like a shadow for several months, confused, unconscious at times, tormented by demons and uncertainties. Finally she died, of hunger and thirst. In death as in life, she was revered throughout Italy, and recognition came early. Within a century of her death, thanks to posthumous miracles, a pope who also hailed from Siena proclaimed her a saint.

WE DO NOT UNDERSTAND ANOREXIA, and we understand Catherine of Siena, whether as a person or an exemplary medieval saint, even less. A clinical examination of her illness, made six centuries later on the basis of what documentation we have, reveals a deeply religious girl in serious conflict with a strong-willed mother who had a large family to manage. When the girl lost sisters of whom she was very fond, she took their place—not as the child of her parents but, rather, as a child of God who rejected the world of marriage and family. In fighting for her convictions, Catherine had to contend with her own needs as well as the pressures of her society. The weapons she chose were starvation, silence, and mortification, and these led her to ecstasy, mystical transports, and assumption into the Holy Family. Outwardly she personified medieval excess, of which flagellation, visions, and the rejection of all things physical were typical. Catherine of Siena thus seems to be a classical example of anorexia nervosa—or, if you will, anorexia religiosa.

Whereas the desire of today's patient to lose weight is dictated by the entirely mundane ideal of thinness, Catherine's wish to be thin was part of her quest for sanctity and withdrawal from the world. Those who believe that anorexia nervosa is a refusal to conform to the behavior of mature womanhood see Catherine's rejection of an arranged marriage as an indication of her desire to remain a child in the Holy Family. Obsession with the maturing body; denial of hunger, thirst, or exhaustion; revolt against parents; erotic fantasies side by side with self-imposed virginity—nothing seems to have changed much over the centuries, only the cultural context in which the anorexia occurs. In a time of plague and armed conflict, of clerical corruption and excess, great value was placed on purity, asceticism, and piety. Today's counterpart is the struggle of Western women, in the midst of plenty, to be thin. Perhaps Buddha is fat because those who worship him do not have enough to eat and are skin and bones. It is certainly true that Miss Universe and all those photographers' models who must stay thin live in a world of overweight people.

But the fact that the affliction is confined mainly to young women may have a feminist explanation: that anorexia is the rejection by women of the role men have assigned them. For devout women in Italy, where ecclesiastical office and the exercise of temporal power are reserved exclusively for men, it could be the ultimate weapon. The only way a woman is able to rebel is by renouncing daily obligations, habits, and obedience in the name of spirituality.

If anorexia is a cultural illness, its frequency should vary as circumstances change. When, after the Middle Ages, the Church set stricter criteria for beatification and rejected self-mortification by starvation or flagellation, the number of anorexic saints appearing on the calendar diminished. In our time, anorexia nervosa seems to be on the rise in affluent circles, during a period when teenagers have greater freedom than ever to express themselves in their dress, behavior, eating preferences, and schooling. The dialectics of Marx, Freud, or feminism must have a problem here drawing historical comparisons.

Physicians, on the other hand, seem to have learned to keep their options open. The most reputable textbooks on internal medicine deal with anorexia nervosa in their chapters on nutrition and describe it, neutrally, as a behavioral disorder that is the most life threatening of the psychiatric afflictions. The definition provided tells what it is not; what it is, is unexplained. Hysteria and the pituitary gland are not in fashion; the causes are pure speculation, the therapy problematical. The psychosomatic diagnosis also falls short—that trendy approach has had its day. That a mental disorder can become physically manifest, in the form of palpitations, insomnia, a high or low threshold of pain, or as the aggravation of an existing physical disorder, has been known since Hippocrates.

Anorexia patients have in common an aversion to food and an obsessive desire to lose weight, but the families in which they are raised differ. Every growing teenager tends to rebel, and no girl wants to be obese. All children are subjected to a variety of social and educational pressures. The parents, the scapegoats of many a psychotherapy, are not invariably the villains and have every right to be concerned when their daughter wants to starve herself to death.

As for Catherine, little of her remains. Saints may not die, but they do fade away. To the current observer, her behavior seems pathological; she would make a good candidate for commitment—which would have done nothing to change her mind. The label of anorexia does not explain much; most saints had poor appetites to begin with. Her severe self-mortification aside, she was passionately involved in the attempt to purge the Church and the clergy, whom she reproached ceaselessly for their dereliction of duty—as Joan of Arc reproached the French king, and Florence Nightingale the British government. In retrospect, Catherine's intervention only hastened the Great Schism, but that does not make her efforts any the less admirable. We no longer comprehend her mystical exaltation, and certainly no one tries to imitate it. The veneration of her as patron saint of Italy stays within narrower limits than the veneration accorded her Umbrian colleague Francis of Assisi, who has been recently rediscovered as the first environmental saint.

Catherine's house and church still stand in Siena. The house contains paintings that illustrate her saintly life—she comforts people condemned to death, exchanges hearts with Christ, receives the crown of thorns, brings the pope back to Rome, and enters into mystical wedlock with Christ. In her church, a simple brick Gothic structure, there are frescoes depicting her in states of ecstasy when she was a sturdy Tuscan farm girl. But these were painted a century and a half after her death. A chapel contains a portrait of her by a contemporary, one Yanni—probably the only authentic portrait—in which, dressed in a Dominican habit, she holds the lily of virginity in her thin, stigmatized hands.

The most ghastly memento, an example of ecclesiastical necrophilism, is her decomposed head, which, along with a severed finger, is displayed in a casket. The rest of the body lies beneath the altar of a church in Rome. The wedding ring—Christ's foreskin—is not available for viewing by skeptics, of course. That privilege was accorded to two devout Frenchwomen praying in the chapel about a century ago. But the limits of credibility are sometimes stretched. Interested persons have since counted nineteen places where Christ's foreskin is preserved.

It is her sheer religious excess that makes it so difficult for us to comprehend Catherine of Siena. All cultures have had those who renounced the world and reached for something above it. The medieval attitude toward the body as a transitory, sinful, and defective vessel for reaching eternity led to attempts to curb the body's greed and lust through fasting and abstinence. In trying to be spiritual, people went to extremes, and Catherine was but one of many. What is striking is not so much the heroic struggle to escape worldly emotions and needs as it is the failure to achieve the ascension through mortification of the flesh. Like gravity, biological life pulls us back to earth, foreskin and all.

Extremes of the Senses

A Taste for Cabin Boys

THE STORY OF Arthur Gordon Pym of Nantucket is a suspenseful ship's-log account of a voyage to the Antarctic in a sailing ship. A mutiny breaks out and, after a great massacre, is quelled by a few survivors. The ship begins to founder during a storm and almost sinks. The four starving survivors see a spectral vessel sail by, laden with corpses. A British schooner finds the men, and they sail on into a fantastic Antarctic world, where most of the crew are murdered by savages. The last survivors reach the South Pole in a large canoe, but are dragged by a maelstrom down into the interior of the earth.

The story takes place in 1827, and it is an amalgam of adventure tale and the science fiction of the day. Many readers were under the impression that Pym's fantastic voyage was true—after all, Antarctica was terra incognita, the farthest limit of the world. The author, Edgar Allan Poe, meant the tale to be read as a symbolic voyage of man in search of extremes. His countryman Herman Melville would follow with *Moby Dick*, the hunt for the great white whale, and Joseph Conrad with his excursion up the Congo, *Heart of Darkness*. All travel is round-trip; the traveler returns to himself.

The Pym story includes supernatural, romantic, and gruesome events, but one in particular stands out. The survivors, adrift in the southern seas in their leaking ship, have nothing left to eat or drink except one bottle of port. After a week of starvation, hallucinations, and apathy, they draw lots. The loser, ship's mate Richard Parker, is cut down and eaten. Poe describes the human sacrifice in vivid detail. Three seamen, all from a puritanical, white, civilized America, consume one of their own in order to survive.

For hundreds of years, travel accounts and letters written during the great voyages of exploration made reference to human sacrifice and cannibalism in strange lands. Spanish priest Bernal Díaz, who in 1518 accompanied Cortés and his 550 soldiers to Mexico in search of Montezuma's gold, reported that nearly all the Spaniards were killed in the expedition and many ended up in an Indian stomach. This was the European view of the new-world savage: a godless, lawless, bloodthirsty, naked cannibal. Which provided an additional motive to subjugate the natives and convert them to Christianity.

Montaigne was among the few who did not believe the tales of barbarism. In his opinion, it was wrong to measure savages by European standards and perceptions; savages were close to nature, lived instinctive, innocent lives, were different from but not inferior to their discoverers. Montaigne considered the consumption of human flesh less heinous than the breaking on the wheel, flaying, and burning alive of condemned persons in Christian Europe.

Cannibalism also occurs in literature, ranging from the *Odyssey* (the giant Polyphemus) to *Robinson Crusoe*. It fascinates because it involves one of the ultimate taboos. The eating of human flesh is a desecration, an abomination often involving idolatry, magic spells, primitivism, and the supernatural. Poe's story is concerned not with savages, however, but with shipwrecked white men who are driven to that extremity out of hunger. One person's self-preservation requires the death of another, and the decision is made that it is better for one to die than for all to be lost. But the consumption of Richard

Parker brings only temporary relief. The rescue of the survivors takes them even farther from civilization, to the very edge of the earth, the dark void of the pole, which, like Hades, swallows everyone who dares to look down into it. Baudelaire read Poe and admired his work and way of life. Baudelaire's translation of the story of Arthur Gordon Pym appeared at the same time as his own volume of poetry, *Les Fleurs du Mal*—two examples of a dark, exotic view of reality.

Reality surpassed fiction with the English sailing yacht *Mignonette*. A crew of four was taking the fifteen-meter yacht around the Cape of Good Hope in 1884, en route from Southampton to a new owner in Australia, when the ship encountered furious winds and storms off Africa and sank in the South Atlantic. The four men saved themselves in their sloop, but had no drinking water or food, and were tossed about without bearings in the shark-infested ocean. The captain, Tom Dudley, did his best to keep the boat seaworthy and his three men alive through the cold nights and scorching days. The young cabin boy, inexperienced and not yet eighteen, was in a bad way. Parched, he had drunk seawater, which made him ill, and diarrhea was aggravating his dehydration. On the fifteenth day, without water and with only a sea turtle for sustenance, the end was near for all of them. There was talk of drawing lots to decide who should die to feed the others—but there was no need to draw lots. The cabin boy, having neither wife nor child, lay sick on the bottom of the boat; he clearly would not survive. The hastening of his death would give his comrades a chance. The captain stabbed the boy in the neck. He bled to death in half a minute, and the blood was collected and drunk. The heart and liver were removed immediately and eaten. Then pieces of flesh were cut from the body, and what remained of the corpse was thrown overboard. The food lasted four days. Finally, after twenty-four days at sea, a German three-master, the *Montezuma*, came into sight and took them on board, and the sloop, too, which still contained a few pieces of flesh. The cabin boy who found a dreadful seaman's grave had the same name as the victim in Poe's story: Richard Parker. When the *Montezuma* docked in England, Dudley and his two crew members were arrested. They had given an open and candid account of what happened, and during the voyage home on the German ship, Dudley had prepared a detailed report that omitted nothing and made no excuses. Richard Parker's family received his back pay. And in the harbor town of Falmouth the extreme act of self-preservation met with little criticism. The men were soon released on bail, and the community showed sympathy and respect for the hardships they had endured. A support fund was established, and the local press treated the shipwreck victims like heroes. The national press followed suit. The minister of the interior, however, had no choice but to direct the public prosecutor to investigate, and the three men were brought to trial. The trial began the same year, 1884, in Exeter, attracting enormous interest from the press, the public, and the legal profession. There were many reasons for the interest, but the most important one probably was the Victorian fascination with murder, violence, and disaster at sea. Not rare occurrences, surely, but the public had an insatiable appetite for every macabre detail.

The trial would inaugurate an enduring tradition of public hypocrisy. People continued to tell themselves that cannibalism was a practice only of savages in remote corners of the British Empire, a practice inconceivable to a civilized seafaring nation—despite the fact that various earlier instances of cannibalism by shipwrecked seafarers were common knowledge. The best-known case was that of the *Medusa*, a French frigate

that went down on the way to Senegal. One hundred and fifty
survivors, starving and ill, clung to a raft. Fights broke out, in
the course of which the weakest were killed and eaten, or cast
into the sea. Only fifteen men lived to tell the tale. Théodore
Géricault did a painting of the tragic raft in 1819; it is one of
the romantic treasures of the Louvre.

In the trial of the *Mignonette* survivors, the basic issue was
whether the killing and the cannibalism were an act of self-
preservation or of murder. The same question had been raised
two centuries earlier by our friend Nicolaas Tulp, who in 1641
published an extensive work on unusual medical experiences.
One, a story he had heard from eyewitnesses, was about seven
Englishmen shipwrecked in the Caribbean. After seventeen days
of drifting, they drew lots to decide who should die to feed
the others. The man who drew the lot was the one who had
proposed the drawing. He was killed, bled, and eaten—all with
rational deliberation. The shipwrecked men eventually landed
on the Dutch island of Saint Martin, received a cordial wel-
come, and were acquitted of manslaughter, on the ground of
unavoidable necessity. Dr. Tulp's account was cited as a legal
precedent in the *Mignonette* trial.

For legal reasons, the proceedings were transferred to London, where they again attracted much attention. The defense
contended that in extreme circumstances the laws governing
a civilized society had no validity, and that unusual events
could drive people to unusual behavior. In addition, there was
the argument of utility, borrowed from the social philosopher
Jeremy Bentham, which said that the welfare of the many was
a higher good than the welfare of the individual. The bench
was nevertheless persuaded that Richard Parker had been murdered, and it passed the death sentence, but with the recommendation that the Crown commute the sentence. The

crime had been condemned, and the criminals were released after six months in prison. The convicted seamen and the judgment passed on them remained the subject of intense public debate, but one year after the ill-fated *Mignonette* had left England the men were back in their homes.

Captain Dudley emigrated to Australia, worked as a sail maker in Sydney harbor, and died there in 1900, one of the first victims of a local epidemic of plague. He was wrapped in canvas containing a disinfectant, his coffin was filled with sulfur, and he was lowered into a deep hole—an outcast on the other side of the world, who had been at the center of on of the most famous trials in Victorian England. In 1984, British jurist Brian Simpson wrote a marvelous account of this confrontation between the principle of self-preservation and the administration of justice, between cannibalism and a civilized system of law that must run its course.

NOT ALL CANNIBALISM arises out of necessity; it sometimes has a ritual nature. The Spaniards who under Cortés conquered Mexico in 1519 encountered a flourishing Aztec culture—a complex culture rich in architecture and art, warlike and religious, but lacking, in the era of Martin Luther and Erasmus, the plow, the wheel, and an alphabet. They worshiped many gods, each with its own cult. To the rain god, children were sacrificed on mountaintops, as Abraham had once tried to offer up Isaac. The fertility goddess was presented with the skins of slain prisoners. Religion was filled with rites and astrological calendars rooted in the myth that life could be perpetuated through human sacrifices. Every year thousands of prisoners, slaves who had been purchased for the purpose, and children were ritually killed and their hearts offered to the gods. When the hearts were removed, dancers often cast the bodies on a burning pyre, and the meat was later eaten.

Anthropologists have speculated that this type of cannibalism, too, might have arisen out of necessity. A fast-growing population in an environment where there was little game and no domestic animals would suffer an acute shortage of protein. The agriculture was insufficient to make up the nutritional lack. Repeated wars, on the other hand, gave the Aztecs a supply of captives suitable both for ritual offerings and the appeasement of hunger, satisfying gods and men alike. Aztec civilization was not primitive, but it was indeed cruel, obsessed with warfare, blood lust, and torture, and it is unlikely that a need for protein was the only motive for cannibalism. But no one will ever know. The Spaniards dispersed the Aztecs and destroyed their culture. What little of it remains has been difficult to interpret.

The word *cannibal* is a corruption of Carib, the name the natives of the Central American coast and islands gave themselves at the time of Columbus. In Spanish, *Carib* became *caribal* or *canibal*. In Shakespeare's last play, *The Tempest*, written after he heard accounts of the great voyages of exploration, the wild magician on the island is called Caliban. These natives were the unknown children of nature who, in Montaigne's opinion, were no less worthy than Europeans. The colonizers thought otherwise after the practice of eating human flesh came to light. To them, *savage* was now synonymous with *cannibal*, and cannibals were to be found everywhere on the periphery of the European expansion—in Central America, Central Africa, the Pacific South Sea islands, and New Zealand. This mythology provided an argument for colonization: the arrival of the white man spelled the end of cannibalism, which would survive only in fairy tales and satires.

Anthropologists have identified different kinds of cannibalism. Endocannibalism is the eating of the flesh of a deceased person by relatives as a token of respect. Exocannibalism is the eating of slaves or prisoners of war. In any case, cannibalism is seldom done for food, for nutritional reasons; it is almost invariably a matter of ritual, and, like ritual murder, involves offerings, head-hunting, or the expropriation of an enemy's strength and spiritual power. Sometimes the mythology of creation and fertility is invoked, of gods who devour mortals and become one with them, as in the Greek legends. Cannibalism then acquires a sacred significance. Did not the medieval mystics and saints in their transports partake of the body of Christ, whose flesh and blood are literally present in the sacrament of the Eucharist? And did not Catherine of Siena, in her hallucinations, drink blood from the wound in the side of the crucified Christ? The sharing of a divine experience is represented, in symbol, in dream, as a physical communion.

There is no adequate explanation for human cannibalism. Anthropologists speak of magic and aggression, protein deficiency and sadism, but the motives and circumstances of cannibalism differ widely. Few savages are left in a world penetrated everywhere by civilization. But it does not follow that ritual human sacrifice no longer exists. It has merely changed its style and dimensions. The altars are now called Gulag, Auschwitz, Cambodia.

SOME LAST REMNANTS of the Stone Age still exist in the eastern mountain regions of New Guinea. The Australians, setting up government there in the 1950s, encountered a strange disease, which in the local vernacular was called kuru, meaning "shivering" or "trembling." It was found to be endemic to the Fore tribe, comprising some tens of thousands of Papuans scattered among two hundred villages. The illness began with impaired muscular coordination, trembling hands and feet, equilibrium problems, and difficulty in walking. By the time it had run its course, the victim was unable to stand, could barely speak or swallow, and usually died of starvation or pneumonia. Women and children were more frequent victims than men. The natives attributed kuru to witchcraft, whose spell could be broken only by ritual murder. The complex of disorders and the slow progression of the illness resembled an advanced form of Parkinson's disease, an affliction in which the degeneration of nerve cells in the brain results in muscular atrophy, tremors, and a shuffling gait. The cause of Parkinson's is unknown, although symptoms can appear after a viral infection or as a side effect of medication. Could the kuru of New Guinea be caused by a virus affecting the brain?

An American researcher, D. C. Gajdusek, had been in Melbourne investigating viral illnesses, with the assistance of his host, Frank Macfarlane Burnet, later a Nobel laureate. Intrigued by what he heard about kuru, Gajdusek stopped in Australian New Guinea on his way home. With Burnet's son, he accompanied a patrol into the interior. The illness seemed to have more in common with hysteria than a brain disorder. But hysteria didn't explain the complete neurological degeneration that followed within six months of the first tremors. Gajdusek decided to stay and do further research. Assiduously, meticulously, he mapped out the clinical picture, and had blood and tissue samples flown to laboratories in Australia. No measles, chicken pox, or whooping cough virus was found; the search for toxic substances also led nowhere. Nor was there evidence of vitamin or protein deficiency, and the native diet contained no toxic metallic acids. Moreover, those who left the tribal area and went to work on the coast could also contract kuru.

None of the experimental treatments with antibiotics, vitamins, adrenocortical hormones, or mineral-compound remedies had any effect, which only made the riddle more baffling. From extensive questioning of the villagers it was learned that the disease had appeared, sporadically, some forty years earlier, but had only now assumed epidemic proportions, and only in a limited area. Where there had been no contact with neighboring tribes, the disease was absent. Women appeared to pass it on to their children, so a genetic cause was likely.

Gajdusek's description of the strange epidemic created considerable interest in professional publications, but none of the researchers who went to the area after he left could come up with a theory. Then a British veterinarian pointed out the similarities between kuru and a sheep's disease called scrapie, which occurred only in particular flocks and was caused by a virus. The impairments of muscular movement were almost identical in the two diseases. When brain tissue from sheep with scrapie was injected into healthy animals, they contracted the disease, but not until two or three years later.

Gajdusek had been looking for a link between a viral disease and kuru, but had not considered the possibility of so long an incubation period. Returning to New Guinea, he obtained brain tissue from deceased kuru victims, and injected this into chimpanzees in the United States. After three years the chimpanzees developed kuru, and Gajdusek filmed them, as he had filmed the Papuans, to show the striking similarities. Kuru was the first disease in which a slow-acting virus was identified as the cause of brain degeneration. Gajdusek finally succeeded in isolating the virus, and in 1976 he was awarded the Nobel Prize in medicine.

But that still did not answer the question of how kuru spread. A husband-and-wife team of anthropologists named

Glass carefully followed Gajdusek's trail through the tribal population. They discovered that in 1915 the tribe had adopted cannibalism in its burial rituals. Organs and muscles were partly roasted or cooked, but especially the brain, and consumed, mostly by the women and children. The male warriors normally abstained. In the children, the disease ran its course rapidly. In older persons, the interval between the funeral meal and the onset of the disease could be several years. Kuru, then, was a contagious viral disease contracted through the consumption of human brain tissue in which the virus lay buried like a time bomb. Kuru would disappear when cannibalism, under the influence of missionaries and the administrative authorities, was abandoned, and this indeed occurred in the ensuing years.

As with the Aztecs, the cannibalism of New Guinea was attributed by some to acute protein deficiency: the eating of deceased relatives being necessary for survival. By which argument, the Papuans were only doing what some shipwrecked British sailors had done. When the burial rituals were completed, the principle of utility became operative—in the same way that a brain-dead person's organs enable others to survive. This relativizing explanation would have satisfied Montaigne. Except that in the tribal conflict in New Guinea, the bodies of slain foes were used not only for food but also as an opportunity for vengeance. Corpses were mutilated, and victors, not to be outdone by Gilles de Rais, flaunted their triumph by having sexual intercourse with the dead. Human bones and pieces of flesh were hung on bushes and in trees to promote the fertility of women and the earth. The extremes of death and eroticism, starvation and violence are sometimes closely related. In such cases, a body of one man no longer serves to sustain the life of another, but becomes simply his victim.

In the Land of the Blind

THE BOY was about three years old at the time of the accident. He was playing in the workshop of his father, a saddler in a French village on the Marne. He was alone, and no one knows exactly what happened. Playing with some tools, he poked himself with an awl or knife in the eye. It was the kind of accident toddlers are prone to, when they are not being watched and are playing with objects meant for adults. The boy's eye was irreparably damaged; the eyeball had been perforated. In 1812, little medical assistance was available in cases of serious injury, and certainly not in the country. Napoleon had set forth on his Russian campaign that summer, and the best doctors were accompanying the army to Moscow. In the absence of any other treatment, people resorted to folk remedies, so the child's eye was dressed with medicinal plasters and herbs. A rare but much feared complication set in, causing blindness in the other eye as well. This might have been due to an infection that spread from the damaged eye or to an unusual immunological response to the infection.

The child was plunged into permanent darkness. The parents, overcome by guilt, did their best to raise the child, but they could see no future for him. The blind did not receive any special assistance in those days, and if they had no family to take care of them, they had to earn their livelihood by begging or being exhibited at fairs. Meanwhile, Napoleon was defeated, leaving France a worn-out country occupied for a time by foreign troops and inundated by the wounded and disabled survivors of the Grande Armée's Russian campaign.

The boy was extremely intelligent and had a cheerful disposition. His saddler father, assisted by the pastor, tried to teach him to read by means of letters made of hobnails hammered into pieces of wood. By touching these "alphabet blocks," the boy learned the letters and a few simple words. His father also taught him to write the letters on paper. But this wouldn't help him with reading or writing in the village school, although he excelled in other subjects by virtue of his exceptionally retentive memory.

The French monarchy was now restored, and the members of the aristocracy who had fled during the Revolution had returned. The new king, specially concerned about the blind, sponsored the establishment in Paris of a Royal Institute for Blind Children, to which each region of France could send one child. The building made available to the institute, located in the Latin Quarter, had been a seminary for priests and was run-down, dark, and damp—but blind children would not notice that. It had also been an orphanage, and Vincent de Paul, the future saint, had lived and worked for his order there in the seventeenth century, providing comfort and relief to the poor, the stricken, and the imprisoned. The building had also witnessed less worthwhile activities. In September 1792, at Marat's behest, street mobs and criminals combed the prisons of Paris for alleged conspirators against the new regime. Half were slaughtered, mutilated, and exhibited to the public in the most bloodthirsty fashion. But 130 of them, young priests, were incarcerated in the old seminary. Then, on the first two days of September of Year 1 of the Republic, nearly all these priests were murdered in an orgy of drunkenness and blood lust born of and nurtured by the Terror.

As a result of the Terror, much of France's limited experience in educating the blind was also lost. In 1771, a young official in Paris had given a few coins to a little blind beggar outside a church. He noticed that the boy fingered the coins to assess their value. The official, Valentin Hauy, thereupon adopted the boy as his "Pygmalion" and devoted the rest of his life to the education of the blind. He began teaching the lad by using blocks of wood with letters carved on them in relief, but these were too crude and primitive for reading purposes. Seeking a better solution, Hauy thought of raised print. If letters could be impressed on strong paper with enough force, they would appear in relief on the other side and fingers could feel them. Something like this might work for many blind people. Hauy immediately started soliciting funds. He opened a small school for the blind in Paris in 1785, with his young pupil as the first teacher. The teaching materials consisted of a dozen books printed with the letters in relief. The Academy of Sciences took an interest, and the pupils even demonstrated their finger reading for Louis XVI and Marie Antoinette. The school was designated a royal institution, although that did not guarantee it any income. Then, during the Revolution, all vestiges of the *ancien régime* were swept away. The school ceased to exist, the blind children were scattered among workhouses and asylums, and the man who had been teaching them fled France.

The reestablishment of an institute for the blind, managed by returned aristocrats and again graced with the designation "royal," took place in 1818. In February 1819, the ten-year-old blind son of the saddler was enrolled as pupil number seventy. His name was Louis Braille. The director of the school, in its run-down old quarters, was extremely frugal, and very strict with his pupils; he drilled them as if they were in reform school. They did not learn much, but music was the director's hobby, and in that the boys were given free rein. For such reading lessons as they got, they had a little material in the relief print, which they ran their fingers across until they could make out words and sentences. It was an extremely slow and laborious procedure, and did not really make reading very accessible to the boys. In truth, the Royal Institute for Blind Children was little more than a workhouse with miserable accommodations and food.

Conditions improved when a gifted young doctor, André Pignier, became director. For twenty years, Pignier would battle indifference and the bureaucracy to get better facilities for his pupils. He was the first to realize that people who could see were poorly equipped to lead the blind, because they could not, or did not choose to, conceive of what it was like not to be able to see. The blind were asked to learn what the nonblind learned, to read the same letters and words but with their fingers rather than their eyes. In this they were making little progress.

Pignier made the acquaintance of an army captain named Charles Barbier, a man with an idée fixe. Soldiers in the field could receive their orders at night not by light signals, which were dangerous, but by coded instructions they could sense with their fingers. Barbier had devised a system of dots and dashes that were impressed on a piece of cardboard by an awl attached to a ruler. The raised surface of dots and dashes on the reverse side of the cardboard, when touched in the dark, gave the code. Barbier called his system *l'écriture nocturne*, night-writing. Neither the army nor scientific circles had shown any interest, so he was bringing his invention to the institute to be tested.

The pupils tackled the task enthusiastically, having little

else to do except go for walks in the botanical garden in good weather, clutching a rope like members of a chain gang. Barbier's new system proved a disappointment. It was a sort of stenography, a phonetic script, a little faster than raised print because of the use of code, but no aid to learning anything because there was nothing written in that code. It could pass on limited information in the dark, but it was totally unsuited to the education of the blind. The inventor maintained until the day of his death, however, that he had solved their reading problem.

Louis Braille learned to put up with his lot; he worked on simple handcrafts, played music, and absorbed what he could from the few books available to him. He was a gifted, industrious pupil who fought the limitations of his handicap. He understood that the touching of letters or codes had to substitute for vision but that their meaning was something apprehended not by the eyes but by the brain. An alphabet that was suitable for fingers, therefore, did not need to be the same as one designed for eyes that could see.

The skin of the fingertips contains a network of receptors that transmit to the brain the position, intensity, and sequence of a tactile stimulus. A fingertip pressure of a few grams per millimeter is enough to cause the sensation of touch. Braille knew from bitter experience that the fingering of large raised letters made hardly any use of this subtle tactile ability. With iron determination, he set about searching for a code that would. He experimented with an awl and heavy paper, producing on the reverse side of the paper a four-dot code that, depending on the number and position of the dots, represented letters. He expanded the code to six dots arranged in three pairs, one below the other, an alphabet of patterns, like dominoes. Perhaps the game of dominoes, popular then in France and Italy, indeed gave him the idea.

Many scientific insights have been based on technological inventions. The fire-engine pump showed Harvey how the blood circulates; the internal-combustion engine would illustrate the cardiac physiology of the twentieth century; and today the computer is used to demonstrate theories about the structure of the human brain. Braille writing was such an invention. At the very beginning of human evolution, the hand was essential as a tool for man the creator, *homo faber*. As time went on, the hand kept its sense of touch but needed it less than it did its manipulative skill, the motor ability to work and gesture. A blind person, undistracted by the dominant sensory information vision provides, "sees" through his hands, and by touch can conjure up a world of associations. The blind have a different and often more developed perception of their environment. They demonstrate the possibilities open to people when the power of sight fails.

Braille's six dots, by their number and arrangement, yielded sixty-three symbols. The dots were about three millimeters apart. A century would pass before neurologists determined that the minimum distance the fingertips are capable of detecting is two millimeters. Six dots represent the maximum amount of information that one fleeting touch can absorb. A sighted person who has seen the Braille system feels only a series of dots and has trouble interpreting them. But a blind Braille reader can take in 60 to 120 words a minute, can translate two to three thousand dots a minute into meaningful sentences. Usually an index finger does the reading, but it can also be a thumb, a toe, even the point of one's nose. The blind reader, just as a person with sight, perceives not individual letters but words, lines of text. His finger touch is the equivalent of the movement of a sighted person's eye, and both finger and eye are in instantaneous communication with the brain's center for the processing of that information.

Almost half a century before Braille, Denis Diderot, editor of the famous *Encyclopédie*, had become interested in deafness and blindness and had made extensive observations about them. He believed that the souls of the blind resided in their fingertips, that their thoughts originated there. Braille's invention demonstrated that eyes and fingertips were organs of perception only and that the faculty of language took place in the brain alone. This empirical discovery of a way to transmit information to the brain through touch gave a reader of Braille the same advantages a sighted reader had. Braille could not have accomplished this without being blind; no sighted person could have had his intuition.

In 1825, Braille and his fellow students, assisted by their director, constructed a small tablet, a simple drawing board over which a ruler was moved, with openings in the ruler through which dots could be printed, in reverse, on the other side of a thick sheet of paper. This writing implement allowed rapid notation that could be read by another blind person with equal speed. It gave the institute an enormous opportunity, but the financial means were lacking.

Braille, blind for fifteen years and a pupil at the institute for eight, now became a teacher in his own school, an arrangement that had important consequences. He was not only an inventor but also proved to be a gifted teacher, always ready to help and completely dedicated to the education of the blind. Wanting his system to become the key to reading and writing for those who could not see, their door to the world, he never stopped working on ways to improve it. It turned out that the system could be used for music notation, too, and Braille became the organist of a church in the neighborhood.

The authorities, however, had no faith in Braille's system, and Captain Barbier claimed it was his night-writing distorted beyond recognition. Braille decided therefore to publicize his invention—in a booklet printed in the outmoded relief-letter method. He described his system of dots produced by ruler and awl in such a manner that both the blind and the nonblind could understand it. At first the booklet attracted little attention. Then, after 1830, when the bourgeois King Louis-Philippe took power, France revived. Visitors came to tour the institute; some of its pupils became teachers at other institutes; and the Braille system was demonstrated at exhibitions and in concerts given by blind musicians. The institute received new recognition and support. It produced a number of books using the new system—books assembled by blind boys in an old reformatory and paid for out of their own pockets. The first Braille book was a brief history of France, printed by hand on thick paper, in three volumes comprising a total of two hundred pages and weighing four and a half pounds.

Yet the bureaucrats, as well as the deputy director of the institute, still believed that for the blind to have a language of their own would only drive them deeper into darkness and isolation. The answer, they thought, lay in the old relief printing, which served both those who could see and those who couldn't. Louis Braille tried to narrow the gap between the two methods, and in this he was assisted by another talented blind man, Pierre Foucault. Together they devised a mechanical typewriter with ten metal fingers that inscribed raised dots on paper. Here was a writing machine available to all the blind. Later, this machine was adapted to produce music notation as well.

In 1844, the Royal Institute for Blind Children was finally given more decent accommodations. At the opening ceremony there was an elaborate demonstration of the Braille system in words and music. Braille himself was present, grateful for the recognition but aware that his days were numbered. Eight years earlier, he had started to cough up blood; the tuberculosis he had contracted during his years of poverty and malnutrition in the damp old building was sapping his remaining strength. When he was up to it, he played the organ in the chapel of the seminary. (The building had been returned to the church.) Mostly, he wasted away in his room. He distributed all his possessions. He told his former director that God had been good to him by permitting him to alleviate the lot of those who shared his misfortune. His blindness, he felt, had been of benefit to his soul. Braille died in January 1852. Both the blind and the nonblind came to pay their respects. A death mask was made for a monument, but the monument was never erected. His body was delivered to his eldest brother and taken back by horse cart to the small country village it had come from. Family members and friends attended the funeral, and Louis Braille, beyond the confines of the institute, remained unknown.

His system would have its followers, but also its detractors, because some begrudged the blind an alphabet of their own. In the United States, different though not better variations were proposed. It was not until 1878 that the countries of Europe decided to adopt the Braille system for the education of the blind. It took until 1912 in America, and Braille's standard use worldwide came decades later, under the aegis of the United Nations and the World Health Organization. Today it is the universal alphabet of 40 million blind persons, and programming and printing technology has made possible many new applications in music and science. The American Helen Keller, blind and deaf from infancy, learned to read and write with Braille, graduated from college cum laude, and devoted her life to the deaf and the blind. On the occasion of the one hundredth anniversary of Louis Braille's death, she wrote that in the Sahara of blindness he had sowed a gift of inexhaustible fertility and joy. It was thanks to him that she had gained access to the world of poetry, history, and literature.

Braille did not become a famous Frenchman like Pasteur or Charcot. Nowhere is there a street or square named after him, nor was there a good biography. That omission has recently been remedied by an Australian journalist, Lennard Bickel, and I have derived many of my facts from his *Triumph over Darkness*. The book shows that Braille was an extraordinary human being, inventive, unselfish, and resolute throughout his brief and poverty-stricken life. The challenge of his blindness led him to extremes of determination and of insight into what the blind needed. It was because of that blindness that he was unknown and unrecognized in the land of the sighted, who, when it was too late, would reflect on the obstacles they had put in his path. He was a minor saint overlooked by Church and state, a poor blind man with tuberculosis who lived in an institution.

So the French state had something to make up for in 1952, on the anniversary of his death. The saddler's cottage in which Braille grew up was restored. In the workshop hangs the tool that blinded him. After a century, the peace of his grave was disturbed and his earthly remains taken in procession to Paris, to be housed in the Pantheon, that former church desecrated by the Revolution and reserved for its great. The honors paid to the first tenants had been inconstant. Marat, for example, the instigator of the September massacres, was carried in triumphantly through the front entrance but removed later by the back door. Braille was given a place beside three naturalists of modest stature, not the company of the great writers of his time, Victor Hugo and Emile Zola.

The village of his birth, Coupvray, unhappy about losing its only famous son to Paris, complained that it was left with an empty grave. A compromise was worked out. The hands whose touch had discovered a new writing were severed and placed in the empty grave, in a small concrete casket. Braille's body was then moved to the basement of the Pantheon, back to oblivion.

False Paradises

THREE SHOTS, badly aimed. Two bullets buried themselves in the wall of the dingy Brussels hotel room; the third struck a young man in the left wrist. But, then, the assailant was drunk—yet not so drunk that he was not shocked at what he had done. Before this, he had written to his wife, his friends, and his mother, that he would do away with himself if his wife, who wanted a divorce, did not return to him. He was twenty-seven years old, the only child of an overprotective mother. His mother, in response to his letter of despair, had promptly come to Brussels. His friend, the victim, had also arrived from London immediately. But the friend refused to stay; it was his threatened departure that occasioned the quarrel and the shooting. The man who fired the shots went in tears to his mother's room to tell her what had happened. Melodramatically he asked his injured friend to go ahead and shoot him. The three of them proceeded to the hospital, where the friend's wound was dressed. The friend wanted to leave. On the way to the railway station, the man insisted that his friend stay. If he did not stay, he would kill him. The friend hailed a policeman. The man was taken into custody. The friend was questioned at the hospital where the bullet had been removed. Three weeks later, the man was found guilty of a misdemeanor, even though the friend did not press charges, and was sent to prison for eighteen months. The friend went home to his mother's farm.

The shots that Paul Verlaine fired at Arthur Rimbaud on July 10, 1873, marked the end of their friendship and the end of Rimbaud's career as a poet. The two would see each other after the sentence was served only once more, in Stuttgart, in an orgy of passion, drunkenness, and violence.

In Verlaine's words, both of them were *poètes maudits*, accursed poets. Verlaine, whose father died young, came from a respectable, strict family and had a rigorous secondary-school education. He became a clerk at the Paris city hall but spent his spare time with poets and writing poetry. He drank, was bisexual, sought the seamy side of life. He achieved recognition with his first poems. When drunk he grew violent at the slightest provocation. In 1870, at the outbreak of the Franco-Prussian War, he married a girl named Mathilde, a sixteen-year-old from a well-to-do family. The young husband joined the citizen militia, began coming home late and intoxicated, and once threatened to strangle his wife and set fire to their home.

A year after the marriage, Verlaine received some poems from a precocious schoolboy, the sixteen-year-old Arthur Rimbaud, who lived in Charleville, an industrial town in northern France. Verlaine invited Rimbaud to Paris, and that visit was the beginning of their friendship. Rimbaud, too, was the child of a strict, domineering mother, who had to raise him, a brother, and two sisters on her own. He was a brilliant student who loved the classics and poetry. In provincial Charleville he felt stifled, believed that only in Paris would he be able to realize his literary aspirations. He ran away from home several times and visited Verlaine, staying with the latter's in-laws. The older, unkempt, and homely Verlaine and the handsome youth soon became lovers, which placed a further strain on Verlaine's new marriage.

Rimbaud was childlike but not innocent. As an adolescent he had been raped by soldiers, and described that humiliation in a poem. He read everything he could find in the Charleville library about magic and alchemy. He wanted to be a visionary, one who through every conceivable distortion of the senses penetrates the unknown. For this he was willing to endure great misery—and in time he would. He became the proponent of a poetry that was all sound and associations, a magical realm of speech-music and symbolism. Little of it was published in his lifetime; publication did not come until long after the shooting incident, through the efforts of his rejected friend Verlaine, after Rimbaud had thrown part of his poems and papers in the fire and begun wandering the world.

Rimbaud's friendship with Verlaine ruined Verlaine's marriage. The two men roamed Paris, smoked hashish, drank absinthe, and had hallucinations. In the summer of 1872, they left Paris and traveled via Belgium to London, where they drifted, under the influence now of alcohol, now of opium. Verlaine was a sentimental, clinging person who wanted Rimbaud all for himself; Rimbaud was a spoiled, stormy adolescent. Their quarrels often led to blows, and both appealed to their mothers. But they always reconciled, until Verlaine, after one silly argument, abandoned his evil genius Rimbaud in London without a cent and took off for Brussels. Then followed the announcement of suicide and the shooting and Rimbaud's wound.

In prison Verlaine was converted to the Catholic faith. Rimbaud meanwhile completed his last prose poem, *Une Saison en enfer*, a reflection on the time he had spent in London with Verlaine (and where Verlaine wrote his famous forlorn lines "*Il pleure dans mon coeur comme il pleut sur la ville.*") *Une Saison en enfer*, in nine chapters, is not easy reading. It describes the poet's descent to hell, and asks what evil is, whether God exists, and how one resigns oneself to life. Rimbaud chooses personal freedom, rejects faith, employment, and everyday existence. The poem is a delirious account of his disillusionment, hallucinations, and failure to reach the unknown through poetry. Finally he gives up; he burns his manuscripts.

Rimbaud then became, in Verlaine's words, a man driven by the wind. With a new friend he wandered through England, until the friend died of typhus. He studied languages in Germany, Italy, and Spain. Occasionally he went home to his mother, but never wrote another poem. The whole of his oeuvre was written between ages fifteen and nineteen, under the influence of absinthe and opium.

In Harderwijk he enlisted in the Dutch colonial army for service in the Far East, sailed to Java, deserted, and returned to France on a British ship. He worked as a construction supervisor in Cyprus, in Aden, became a trader in Ethiopia, initially in coffee and hides, then later in arms and slaves. He lived with an Ethiopian girl, later with a servant. He was a poor businessman, but respected. His poetry, a forgotten drunken episode in his life.

Rimbaud, developing a knee infection which was suspected to be bone cancer, returned to France and his family. His mother was indisposed, but his sister Isabelle was sympathetic and nursed him. The numbness grew worse, and the pain, and he hallucinated under the influence of sleeping potions, fever, and poppy tea. Isabelle arranged a deathbed conversion during his last weeks of delirium, and his mother an honorable burial in Charleville. The rebel and wanderer, magician and evil genius, had returned to his faith and a family grave; the drunken ship was at anchor in the harbor it left.

Rimbaud's legacy is unclear. French is no longer a universal language, and each person who reads the work of this obscure prodigy will interpret his symbols differently. The fascination with Rimbaud's poetry and life endures, but endures as an enigma of the past.

VERLAINE LEFT PRISON a Catholic. For a few years he taught in England and France and led a well-regulated life, although without his wife and child. At heart he wanted to return to his mother in Paris, but in his efforts to find employment there, his prison record pursued him. He drank, roamed, tried to make up with his wife, but she demanded a divorce. He threatened to kill her, and that cost him a second term in jail. He drifted around Paris as a *clochard*, a vagrant, the mascot of artists who called themselves the Decadent Ones. In poor health and indigent, he was often saved by one of the great municipal hospitals of Paris, whose doctors gave the celebrated derelict good care. *Bonheur, Amour*, and *Sagesse* were the titles of his books of poems—marvelous flowers of life's evil.

His work became known, and he continued to write, holding court in his favorite café. He had affairs simultaneously with two women and a man—a successor to Rimbaud—to whom he dedicated volumes of poetry, some of it pornographic. The women, both prostitutes, sold his poems for cash and alternately pampered and rejected him.

At the end of 1892, Verlaine went, by invitation, to the Netherlands for two weeks, where painters and poets respectfully paid him honor; he gave a few unintelligible readings in Amsterdam, the Hague, and Leiden. The sentimental jailbird, wearing the scars of his life, aroused both disgust and admiration. Richer by 900 francs, he returned to Paris. All he remembered of the Netherlands was the girls in the red-light district of Amsterdam, although, with a great deal of help, he managed to publish an account of the trip. He repeated his public readings in Belgium, England, and France. But when a vacancy occurred in the Académie Française, he received not a single vote. Outside the academy, however, he was the prince of poets.

The two women with whom he lived looked after him at times affectionately, at times reluctantly. When he was not in the hospital, he subsisted on welfare. His last literary effort: a foreword to the collected poems of Rimbaud, published twenty-four years after the poets' first meeting. In December 1895, Verlaine contracted pneumonia. Only fifty-one years old, he died of it three weeks later, in delirium, after receiving the last rites.

Verlaine was a legend in his lifetime, as much for his conduct as for his poetry. The friend and lover he had shot would become a legend, too, largely because of Verlaine's efforts to get his work published. But while Rimbaud remains a mysterious alchemist who attempted to transmute the lead of language into the gold of new experience, Verlaine is an accessible poet, more musical, more melancholy, and with better technique. His impressionist use of sound and color makes his poems suitable for setting to music. That is what Debussy proceeded to do.

TWO *poètes maudits*. But not so much doomed poets as poets of doom, composers of satanic verse. Their model was Charles-Pierre Baudelaire, whose only volume, *Les Fleurs du mal*, had been banned after publication on grounds of blasphemy and immorality. Baudelaire was a poet of decadence, the big city, and exotic women, and he had ruined his life in much the same way as they would, dying of syphilis at forty-six, an embittered derelict.

The syphilis that affected his heart valves, spine, and brain had claimed other poets. Alfred de Musset, the great romantic, had valves so leaky that at each heartbeat his head bobbed in time with his pulse. In French cardiology, the *signe de Musset* is the definitive characteristic of syphilis of the aortic valves. Heinrich Heine wasted away for years in his tomb of Parisian mattresses, the victim of syphilitic spinal deterioration. Friedrich Nietzsche developed dementia praecox, syphilitic delusions of grandeur. As for Baudelaire, he became paralyzed and lost his voice a year before his death. The famous internist William Osler would write: Those who serve the gods of Bacchus and Venus do not reach sixty.

In the form and content of his work, Baudelaire was the first of those modern French poets who found their inspiration in the gutters of the big city. Like Rimbaud and Verlaine, he sought experience beyond the ordinary, and tried to open wider the doors of poetic perception with the aid of hashish, opium, and absinthe. The pilgrimage to the outer limits could not be made without a complete commitment.

Opium was a popular remedy in the nineteenth century, the aspirin of the day; used for a variety of aches and pains, given to children to keep them quiet, inexpensive and available in every pharmacy. It was sold in the form of a solvent, a brownish-red fluid, under the name of laudanum. Hardly anyone was concerned about its habit-forming property. Laborers used it as a pick-me-up. And for those weary of life, it purchased an easy end. English authors De Quincey and Coleridge, both opium addicts, described their visions: somber landscapes similar to Piranesi engravings, dungeons in the deepest shade of black.

In *Confessions of an English Opium-Eater*, De Quincey spoke of the effects the drug had on his powers of imagination, on his dreams, which were the raw material for his literary creations. He praised opium as the true religion of the romantic imagination, for it opened vistas of unknown worlds. De Quincey had followers. Only later did he mention the addiction, the withdrawal, the trauma. But, an addict, he was hardly an objective observer. What he gained in inspiration and revelation outweighed, for him, the misery of the drug.

His was the first detailed account, by an addict, of the experience. Baudelaire followed, in 1860, with his short book on false paradises. It is a meticulous description of his visions while under the influence of hashish: the concentration on insignificant detail; the dilation of time and space; hallucinations that contained waterfalls, fountains, waves. From this Baudelaire acquired a new awareness of color, shape, and sound, a heightening of all his senses. He usually took the hashish in the company of friends, and followed it with opium, which relieved the abdominal cramps caused by his syphilis. He preferred opium to hashish; his opium dreams, filled with gloomy albeit singular landscapes reaching off into the distance, were more creative. Which confirmed the observations of De Quincey, whom he greatly admired. For Baudelaire, drugs were a way to escape reality for a few hours and reach paradise. It proved to be a false paradise. The enhancement and expansion of the senses in delirium for the purpose of stimulating the poetic imagination were followed by disenchantment. Genuine creative ability was indispensable. Hashish and laudanum could not provide it; they were, as Poe observed, himself an addict, no more than working tools. Baudelaire eventually rejected the false paradise, but by then it was too late.

He was not the only artist to reach this truth. Hector Berlioz, in his *Symphonie Fantastique*, describes in music his hopeless love for an English actress. In despair, the lover takes an overdose of opium and dreams that he has murdered his beloved and will die on the scaffold. The dream concludes with a witches' sabbath and the *Dies Irae*—orgy and judgment combined.

BOTH AS POET and in his precise descriptions of his ecstatic state, Baudelaire influenced the lives and work of later poets. Verlaine attended his idol's funeral, in 1867, and five years afterward he and Rimbaud were drifting, drinking, and smoking opium, a habit they probably picked up from Chinese harbor workers in London. Rimbaud's quest for paradise, for the magic of poetry, became a season in hell, while Verlaine sought his paradise in sexual excess and the consumption of absinthe, the green enchantress.

Absinthe is a distillation of the leaves and flowers of the wormwood shrub, or artemisia. It is astringent, green in color, and around 1840, was added to the wine of French soldiers during the colonial war in Algeria, possibly as an antidote to fever. In the latter half of the nineteenth century, it became an enormously popular drink in France and Switzerland. The firm of Pernod, in the French Jura, added it to grain alcohol. This bitter liqueur was drinkable only when mixed with cold water poured over a few sugar lumps, which turned it cloudy. The "green hour" became a routine of Parisian café life, and Manet, Degas, Daumier, and Picasso often painted absinthe drinkers, as characterizing the seamier side of the city—the new theme in art. Van Gogh, once sketched by Toulouse-Lautrec holding a glass of absinthe in his hand, painted a serene still life of a glass and carafe of absinthe.

As we have since learned, pure absinthe is toxic. It was frequently mixed with other herbs, but also with copper and antimony salts, to get the much-desired green hue, and with methanol, the poison of spirit drinkers. Experiments with laboratory animals and the mentally retarded have revealed that absinthe, when consumed undiluted by alcohol, can induce hallucinations and fits resembling the symptoms of epilepsy. But the medical warnings were ignored, for commercial reasons, and production of absinthe in France was not prohibited until 1915.

In chemical structure and effect, absinthe resembles camphor. It stimulates the central nervous system and causes hallucinations and convulsions. But, as with many addicts today, it is impossible to separate the effects of alcohol, drugs, and privation. Although millions of the French consumed absinthe liqueur in moderate amounts, some artists became obsessed with it because of the intoxication it produced—an enchanting and prolonged distortion of the senses.

For Rimbaud, absinthe was a means of reaching the unknown. His *Comédie de la Soif* tells of his search for the green pillars of the Temple of Absinthe. It ends in disillusionment —as did his poetic career, compressed into four youthful years of dissolution, with the gunshots in Brussels.

Baudelaire was a disappointed man—as poet and as drug user. His analysis of false paradises showed that drugs were not the path to art or freedom. He had little time left. Discouraged, casting about for a source of income, he gave lectures about his experiences with opium and hashish to the Belgians, whom he despised. They showed little interest, and only the unknown twenty-one-year-old Verlaine, in a number of articles, praised him. Soon afterward the fatal phase of his illness, which led to mental and physical paralysis, set in.

Verlaine became an alcoholic, an apostle of the green fairy, nodding over his absinthe, frequently hospitalized, in violent conflict with his environment. He was the vagabond poet who dreamed of "*l'inflexion des voix qui se sont tues*," the voices of his mother, his wife, and his friend and lover, but also the voice of the muse—all of whom had abandoned him in the city, where it rained on the streets and in his heart. On his deathbed the prodigal son cursed absinthe and alcohol.

Baudelaire, Rimbaud, and Verlaine were innovative, exotic poets in their language, subject matter, and symbolism. They were poets of a new relationship with reality, of doors opening to a heightened perception. It is questionable, however, whether opium, hashish, absinthe, or alcohol made any real contribution to this. The references in their works to the effects of these intoxicants are really symbols of the landscape of the soul and not realistic descriptions. For all three men, addiction ended in misery, illness, and remorse, a paralysis not only of the will but of their art. The flowers of evil bloomed in spite of self-toxication rather than because of it.

Their poetry is called modern because it breaks with romantic lyricism. Their lives—the metropolitan milieu, the wandering, the sordidness, the constant need for money, the encounters with the law and the press—made them notorious. Subsequent generations, on a much larger scale but by similar means, would also try to heighten experience, would make pilgrimages to the Orient, would cross the frontiers of heroin or cocaine, incurring the same violence, disease, and degeneration—with syphilis replaced by AIDS.

Osler, who was cited earlier, bequeathed to the medical world a number of down-to-earth aphorisms; they were written around 1900. Besides being a great clinician and teacher, he was a man of artistic sensibility and well aware of the limitations of his profession. One of his aphorisms says that half of us are blind, all of us are deaf, and few have a heart, and this applies not only to medicine but to music, literature, and painting, too. He also wrote that human beings differ from animals only in their persistent desire to take pills.

The physician has a different perception of reality than

the poet does. From the wormwood shrub that yields absinthe, new antimalarial remedies are currently being developed. Perhaps the French colonial troops in Algeria in 1840 benefited in an unsuspected way from the bitterness added to the wine in their military flasks. Syphilis is now effectively controlled by penicillin. Morphine is obtainable only by prescription, although one can buy hashish in many a coffee shop in Amsterdam.

The *jeunesse dorée* of the West, without Baudelaire's flowers, Rimbaud's revelations, or Verlaine's romances *sans paroles*, begins its own search for new experiences. But alcohol and drugs do not produce poetry. As Baudelaire said, they are poor surrogates for the yearning for what is eternal, surrogates taken in the desire to regain immediately a lost paradise, even if the paradise regained proves to be a hell.

References

The Burning Heart

Beguin, A. *Pascal par lui-même*. Paris, 1952.

Berents, D. A. *Guilles de Rais, de moordenaar en de mythe*. The Hague, 1982.

Chavardès, M. *Montaigne*. Paris, 1972.

Montaigne, Michel Eyquem de, *Essais*. Paris, 1962.

Pascal, Blaise. *Pensées*. Paris, 1976.

Reliquet, P. *Le Moyen Age: Gilles de Rais*. Paris, 1982.

Rümke, H. C. *Op de drempel*. Amsterdam, 1965.

Tournier, Michel. *Gilles et Jeanne*. Paris, 1983.

Warner, M. *Joan of Arc: The Image of Female Heroism*. London, 1981.

Heart Transplants

Ladama, J. *Sainte Marguérite-Marie et la visitation de Paray*. Paray-le-Monial, 1977.

Leibowitz, J. O. *The History of Coronary Heart Disease*. Berkeley, Calif., 1970.

Lewinsohn, R. *Eine Weltgeschichte des Herzens*. Hamburg, 1959.

Mannebach, H. *Hundert Jahre Herzgeschichte*. Berlin, 1981.

Van den Berg, J. H. *Het menselijk lichaam*, vols. I and II. Nijerk, 1958 1961.

The Neurotic Heart

Gay, Peter. *Freud; A Life for Our Time*. New York, 1988.

Jones, Ernest. *The Life and Work of Sigmund Freud*. New York, 1955.

Kuehn, J. L. "Encounter at Leyden: Gustav Mahler Consults Freud," *Psychoanalytical Review*, 52:345, 1965.

Lebrecht, Norman. *Mahler Remembered*. London, 1987.

Levy, D. "Gustav Mahler and Emanuel Libman: Bacterial Endocarditis in 1911," *British Medical Journal*, 293:1628, 1986.

Mahler, Alma. *Mein Leben*. Frankfurt am Main, 1960.

Mitchell, Donald. *Gustav Mahler*. Berkeley, Calif., 1975.

Müller, K. J. *Mahler: Leben—Werke—Dokumente*. Mainz, 1988.

Reeser, F. *Gustav Mahler und Holland*. Vienna, 1980.

Roazen, Paul. *Freud and His Followers*. New York, 1971.

Soldier's Heart

Lewis, Thomas. *The Soldier's Heart and the Effort Syndrome*. London, 1918.

Middlebrook, N. *The First Day on the Somme*. London, 1971.

Paul, O. "Da Costa's Syndrome or Neurocirculatory Asthenia," *British Heart Journal*, 58:306–15, 1987.

Sassoon, Siegfried. *Selected Poems*. London, 1968.

Winter, Denis. *Death's Men: Soldiers of the Great War*. London, 1978.

Wood, P. *Diseases of the Heart and Circulation*. London, 1968.

The Perfect Crime

Arasse, Daniel. *De machine van de revolutie*. Nijmegen, 1989.

Bonnet, J. C. *La mort de Marat*. Paris, 1986.

Cabanès, A. *Le cabinet secret de l'histoire*, dl. 3. Paris, 1925.

Clark, Kenneth. *The Romantic Rebellion*. London, 1973.

Loomis, Stanley. *Paris in the Terror*. London, 1965.

Schama, Simon. *Citizens: A Chronicle of the French Revolution*. New York, 1989.

The Anatomy Lesson

~~Broos, B. *Meesterwerken in het Mauritshuis*. The Hague, 1987.~~

De Moulin, D., Eeghen, I–II, R. van Meischke. *Vier eeuwen Amsterdams Binnengasthuis*. Wormer, 1981.

Fuchs, R. M. *Rembrandt en Amsterdam*. Rotterdam, 1968.

Lindeboom, G. A. *De geschiedenis van de medische wetenschap in Nederland*. Bussum, 1972.

Richardson, Ruth. *Death, Dissection and the Destitute*. London, 1987.

Richardson, R., and B. Hurwitz. "Jeremy Bentham's Self-Image: An Exemplary Bequest for Dissection," *British Medical Journal*, 295:195, 1987.

Schwartz, A. *Rembrandt, zijn leven, zijn schilderijen*. Amsterdam, 1984.

Eternal Youth

Altman, Lawrence K. *Who Goes First? The Story of Self-Experimentation in Medicine*. New York, 1981.

Borell, M. "Brown-Séquard's Organotherapy and Its Appearance in America at the End of the Nineteenth Century," *Bulletin of the History of Medicine*, 50:309–21, 1976.

Lock, S. " 'O That I Were Young Again': Yeats and the Steinach Operation," *British Medical Journal*, 287:1964–68, 1983.

Lüth, P. *Geschichte der Geriatrie*. Stuttgart, 1965.

Voronoff, S. *Etudes sur la vieillesse et le rajeunissement par la greffe*. Paris, 1926.

"Viva il Coltello"

Bouvier, R. *Farinelli, le chanteur des Rois*. Paris, 1943.

Christiansen, Rupert. *Prima Donna*. Oxford, 1984.

Einstein, Alfred. *Mozart: His Character, His Work*. Oxford, 1945.

Heriot, Angus. *The Castrati in Opera*. London, 1956.

Pleasants, H. *The Great Singers*. New York, 1966.

Parthenogenesis

Crews, D. "Courtship in Unisexual Lizards: A Model for Brain Revolution," *Scientific American*, Dec. 1987, p. 116.

Johnson, Paul. *A History of Christianity*. London, 1981.

Pagels, Elaine. *The Gnostic Gospels*. New York, 1981.

Warner, Marina. *Alone of All Her Sex: The Myth and the Cult of the Virgin Mary*. London, 1978.

Warner, M. *Monuments and Maidens: The Allegory of the Female Form*. London, 1985.

Heretics

Cohn, Norman. *Europe's Inner Demons*. Sussex University Press, 1975.

Lea, Henry C. *De inquisitie in de middeleuwen*. Utrecht, 1966.

Moore, R. I. *The Formation of a Persecuting Society*. Oxford, 1987.

Nelli, Rene. *Les Cathares*. Paris, 1972.

Niel, P. *Albigeois et cathares*. Paris, 1982.

Anorexia Religiosa

Bell, Rudolph M. *Holy Anorexia*. Chicago, 1985. *Sancta Anorexia: Vrouwelijke wegen naar heiligheid, Italy,* 1200–1800. Amsterdam, 1990.

Farmer, C. H. *The Oxford Dictionary of Saints*. Oxford, 1982.

Huizinga, Johan. *Herfsttij der Middeleeuwen*. Zwolle, 1952.

Rudofsky, B. *The Unfashionable Human Body*. New York, 1974.

Van Deth, R., and Walter Vandereycken. *Van vastenwonder tot magerzucht*. Meppel, 1988.

A Taste for Cabin Boys

Bray, Warwick. *Everyday Life of the Aztecs*. London, 1968.

Díaz, B. *The Conquest of New Spain*. London, 1963.

Farb, P., and G. Armelagos. *Consuming Passions: The Anthropology of Eating*. Washington, D.C., 1980.

Gajdusek, D. C. "Unconventional Viruses and the Origin and Disappearance of Kuru," *Science*, 197:943–60, 1977.

Howell, M., and P. Ford. *The Ghost Disease*. London, 1986.

Poe, Edgar Allan. *The Narrative of Arthur Gordon Pym of Nantucket*. London, 1975.

Thornsen, C. W. *Menschenfresser*. Vienna, 1983.

In the Land of the Blind

Bickel, Lennard. *Triumph over Darkness*. Sydney, 1988.

Critchley, Macdonald. *The Citadel of the Senses*. New York, 1986.

Foucault, Michel. *Naissance de la clinique*. Paris, 1963.

False Paradises

Benjamin, W. *Charles Baudelaire, ein Lyriker im Zeitaler des Hochkapitalismus.* Frankfurt am Main, 1955.

Conrad, Barnaly. *Absinthe: History in a Bottle*. San Francisco, 1988.

Hayter, Alethea. *Opium and the Romantic Imagination*. London, 1968.

Heybroek, J. F., and A. A. M. Vis. *Verlaine in Nederland*. Amsterdam, 1985.

Petitfils, Pierre. *Album Verlaine*, Paris, 1981.

Spaans, I. *Arthur Rimbaud, Paul Verlaine, een geschreven vriendschap*. Amsterdam, 1985.

Starkie, Enid. *Arthur Rimbaud*. London, 1961.

ACKNOWLEDGMENTS

I AM GRATEFUL to a number of critical readers in my circle of colleagues, friends, and experts, who pointed out my errors. For the blind spots that remain, I am solely responsible.

I am particularly indebted to Mrs. Yvonne Nauta-Durrer for all her patient and cheerful assistance, and to my colleague Noud Vroom, who during the last weeks of his life read through the manuscript with great care.

The staff of the *Nederlands Tijdschrift voor Geneeskunde* (Netherlands Medical Journal) was helpful in tracking down source material from the historical library.